A GUIDE
TO ORGANIZING
MISSIONS AND
EVANGELISTIC ACTIVITIES
. . . WITH A LITTLE
FORETHOUGHT.

Scripture Union
130 City Road, London EC1V 2NJ

British Youth for Christ
Cleobury Mortimer, Kidderminster DY14 8JG

DEDICATED TO MY FAMILY

To my father and mother, Ron and
Doreen, whose love and care
enabled me to follow Jesus.

To my wife, Sue, who believes in
me and who loves me regardless.

To our son, Ian, whom we love
and hope that he will hear and
respond to the Good News of
Jesus.

© Malcolm Egner 1990

First published 1990

**British Library Cataloguing in
Publication Data**
Egner, Malcolm
   Mission: Possible
   1. Christian mission
   I. Title
   266

ISBN 0 86201 554 5

All Scripture quotations in this
publication are from the Holy
Bible, New International Version.
Copyright © 1973, 1978, 1984
International Bible Society.
Published by Hodder and
Stoughton.

Cover and book design by Tony
Cantale Graphics. Cover
photograph by Mick Rock.

The song quoted on page 5 is
copyright © 1983 River Oaks
Music Company (Tree
Group)/Shepherd's Fold
Music/Word Music (UK). Used
by permission.

Printed and bound in Great Britain
by Cox and Wyman Ltd., Reading

| ACKNOWLEDGEMENTS |

No book is written entirely by one person: there are those who inspire, advise and help practically. I would like to thank the following people who have each made valuable contributions, knowingly or otherwise:

John Allan, Christian Szurko and **Pete Gilbert**, who each profoundly influenced my approach to evangelism; and John in particular helped at the outset of this project.

John Graham and **James Sequeira**, who painstakingly worked through the early manuscripts.

Lowell Sheppard, Roy Crowne and **Ian Savory** (BYFC Missions Dept); **Cathie Smith** (SU Missions); **Martin Bluemel**, **John Buckeridge, Ken** and **Lesley Davis**: who between them made useful comments and suggestions on the contents.

Amstrad who produced a cheap miracle (PCW 8256); **David Aitken** who loaned one such machine and quickly relinquished ownership.

Campbell Grant who advised and encouraged, and helped me to be more positive!

The leadership team of **Welwyn Hatfield Youth For Christ**, especially **John Berry**, who encouraged me to develop my writing and allowed me time to work on the book.

Our prayer partners **John** and **Alison, Pete** and **Sue** – a constant source of love and encouragement. Above all, my wife **Sue**, whose confidence in me has never wavered, and whose love and support through a difficult period in our lives has never faltered.

To you all, my heartfelt thanks.

Malcolm Egner

| CONTENTS |

FOREWORD

We are called to take His light to a world where
wrong seems right;
What could be too great a cost for sharing life
with one who's lost?
Through His love our hearts can feel all the grief they bear.
They must hear the words of life only we can share.

People need the Lord. People need the Lord.
At the end of broken dreams – He's the open door.
People need the Lord. People need the Lord.

Almost every Christian believes these words in theory! Many of us
have been stirred again and again by a preacher, personal testimony
or book into recommitting our lives to the evangelistic task. Hardly
any one of us needs convincing that telling other people about Jesus
is an important part of the Christian life. But knowing it is one thing,
doing something about it is quite another!

For most Christians evangelism is done in short, sharp bursts of
enthusiasm, followed by months (or even years) of non-activity. It is
only with a supreme effort of the will (aided by some feelings of
guilt!) that we manage to sustain even the few bursts of enthusiasm
we can muster up.

This rash of enthusiasm usually succeeds in convincing a few non-
Christians that we really are an odd bunch and has very little long-
term effect on the kingdom.

We desperately need a consistent plan for regular, personal, evangelistic activity. We also need to be made aware that we are not alone in this task but are part of local groups of believers who are making a much greater impact corporately than we ever could on our own. This book helpfully illustrates both these emphases. It sets out plans for thorough, church-based evangelism in which every individual must play their part. It carefully helps us to develop workable strategies and pinpoint areas of potential weakness in our planning.

Mission: Possible comes not simply from Malcolm Egner's heart but out of the experience of a man who has been deeply involved in evangelistic activity. Both the organizations involved in publishing this book (Scripture Union and British Youth for Christ), have a growing reputation as servants to the local church. This is no hit-and-run evangelistic approach. Rather, it is a tool to help churches get serious about evangelism.

This book is dangerous because it demands a response. It is uncomfortable because it demands hard work. It is challenging because it constantly reminds us of the need for prayer and openness to God as a prerequisite to any successful strategy. I recommend it as an antidote to apathy and a starting point for a church that is tired of talking about evangelism and actually wanting to do some.

Stephen Gaukroger

PROLOGUE

The impeccably dressed man walked purposefully across the road. He opened the telephone kiosk and stepped inside. With deft movements of the hands he removed the metal covering to reveal a miniature tape machine and an envelope. He switched on the tape:

'Good morning Mr Phelps.

'For many centuries Britain has been known as a Christian country despite an undercurrent of paganism. During the last few decades the church has faced the onslaught of secularization and unbelief, and has been in continuous decline since the late 1920's.

'The High Command has issued instructions to turn the tide by a major mobilization of the church.

'Your mission, should you choose to accept it, is to organize your church into an effective unit in the evangelization of this country. The message you have to proclaim is found in The Book; the most powerful weapon at your disposal is love. The enclosed instructions will provide valuable help.

'This tape will self-destruct in five seconds.'

INTRODUCTION

Why write a book on organizing evangelistic activities?

The short answer is that despite numerous books on specific aspects of evangelism there did not appear to be one that was all-encompassing and that would act as a basic handbook for both new and experienced organizers. The long answer requires a little background painting.

Since I professed my Christian faith publicly through believers' baptism at the age of fourteen, practically every activity with which I have been involved has been geared to evangelism. Such enthusiasm for outreach did not go down too well with the local inter-church youth council but nothing would deter me. On leaving unversity I began a seven-year stint with Youth For Christ, involved in youth evangelism in various parts of the country. Even though I no longer work for a Christian organization I am still heavily involved in outreach through the planting of a congregation in our town. In fifteen years of evangelistic endeavours I have learnt many lessons and made many mistakes, but above all else I have been convinced that God's greatest desire is to see all people come into the love and security of his family.

My desire is to see the church active and effective in outreach. I want to encourage evangelism throughout the church. You can imagine my frustration when I see so much outreach failing to be effective owing to the same mistakes being made time and time again. If only there was some way of encouraging Christians to think through all that is involved in organizing evangelistic activities. If only there was some way of helping them to avoid the pitfalls and to learn from the lessons that I and many others have learnt. My firm hope is that this book will go some way towards fulfilling this desire.

This book is not a blueprint for success in evangelism. Every situation is different. Ultimately, only the Holy Spirit can guarantee 'success'. On the human level, though, effective planning and organization are key factors in our outreach. Our effectiveness can be improved with a little forethought. *Mission: Possible* will help you to think before you act. If you are new to organizing outreach activities you will find all you need to know in order to plan and organize events and missions. If you already have some experience, you will be able to improve your effectiveness by looking in detail at some of the issues which need to be tackled both in theory and in practice.

Some issues are mentioned in passing but cannot be covered in detail in the text. In those cases Appendix 5 gives suggestions for further reading.

If you have scanned the contents page (or if, as many people do, you have read most of the book before coming to the introduction!) you may be wondering why the book is arranged in this order. There are very good reasons and they reflect my particular concerns about evangelism. Firstly, I believe that prayer and personal witness are vital prerequisites to planning a programme, hence they form the foundation of the book. Secondly, we need to recognize that evangelism is a process and therefore full preparations must be made. We must answer the questions: Who are we trying to reach? Who is going to reach them? How? We look at these preparations in Part Two. This explains why the 'nitty-gritty' of organizing is left to Part Three, but even here you may find the chapter order perplexing. Why put follow-up before dealing with the actual event? The answer is because so often this aspect of evangelism is tagged onto the end of the planning process, and is sometimes forgotten altogether. This is a travesty. Follow-up is the most important part of evangelism. Jesus commands us to 'make disciples' and that should be our priority rather than just putting on a good show. Hence follow-up is at the forefront of the 'Practicalities'. Counselling at events, another vital link in the process of evangelism, is also given a complete chapter.

At no stage did I intend this book to be purely theoretical. It is a call to action, so I have concluded each chapter with an action sheet to encourage readers to put theory into practice and work through some of the issues raised.

ACTION SHEETS

The action sheets contain activities which can be used by individuals or groups. Their purpose is twofold:
1. To work through the concepts and principles examined in the chapter.
2. To prepare for action.

Although they are designed primarily for groups of people intending to involve themselves in evangelism and its organization (possibly an evangelism co-ordination group or similar), some sheets, chapters 1 and 2 in particular, will be suitable for other groups such as housegroups. Most of the exercises can be worked through by individuals, too, with minimal adaptation, so it does not matter if there is no evangelism group in your church.

Each action sheet is presented as a complete session, with times shown for each exercise, adding up to between forty-five and ninety minutes for each session. This should be seen as an estimated minimum: groups working together may need to extend the time allowed. Some action sheets are divided into parts, each part being a self-contained session, so that two meetings will probably be needed to cover the material.

Although the action sheets have been designed as complete sessions, each relating to a particular chapter, you need to be aware of their flexibility. You may want to read the whole book before working through any of the exercises. You may prefer to dip in and out of the sheets using a selection of the exercises. You may want to read the book piecemeal – a chapter followed by an action sheet. This is fine. The instructions, too, can be adapted as the situation requires. The main point is to work through the material thoroughly, in whatever way helps you to get the most out of it.

If a group is involved, it is important that every member participates in the exercises. The leader will need to ensure that this happens. If group members do not find it easy to be forthcoming with responses, they may need some encouragement. Ask them to write down their responses in words, or even pictures. After they have done so, ask them to talk about what they have put down. It is often easier to talk about something that you have written or drawn than to make a verbal response from cold. This is especially true of expressing feelings. There is a wealth of material available on leading small groups. Leaders may find it helpful to read some of it.

Eg Leaders' Guide to *Caring for New Christians* (see Appendix 3) or *Small Group Evangelism*, Richard Peace, p84f (see Appendix 5).

1

PREREQUISITES

ITS MISSION:
TO BOLDLY GO
THE NEED FOR PRAYER AND ACTION

'Go and make disciples of all nations, baptising them
in the name of the Father and of the Son and of the Holy Spirit,
and teaching them to obey everything I have commanded you.'
(MATTHEW 28:19, 20)

Jesus' words to his followers shortly before his ascension marked the
start of the expansion of Christianity throughout the world. Over
the next few days 120 disciples gathered in the upper room waiting
for the power that Jesus had promised. Their number grew to 3000
when the Holy Spirit fell on them during the Pentecost celebrations.
Within a few weeks that had become well over 5000, and numbers
continued to increase rapidly. Persecution scattered the Christians
throughout Judea and into Asia Minor, where churches were soon
established. The Christian faith spread throughout the Roman
Empire, and proceeded to dominate European history for the next
two millenia. As Europeans settled in Africa, America and the Pacific
area, so Christianity spread worldwide to become the dominant
religion.[1] The Great Commission that Jesus gave to his disciples was
being fulfilled.

Today, Christianity continues to grow. Since 1970, it has kept
pace with the increasing world population. According to *Barrett's
World Christian Encyclopedia*, 33% of the world's populace profess a
Christian commitment. Christianity is the world's largest religion.

THE SITUATION IN BRITAIN

This is the world picture, but what of the church in Britain? A country in which Christianity is the state religion. A country which has a strong missionary tradition. A country in which the coinage declares that the monarch is the Defender of the Faith, and rules by the grace of God. The situation could not be more different.

The Christian church in Britain is in decline. The number of people in church membership has fallen from 8.06m in 1975 to 7.05m in 1985[2]. Over the same period the population of Britain has increased, so in percentage terms the decline is even greater (figure 1a).

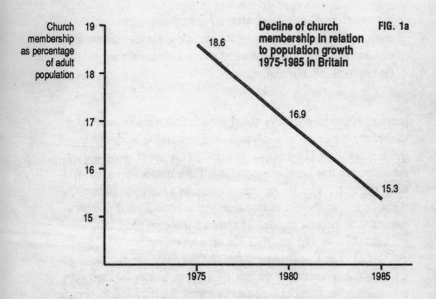

Church membership as percentage of adult population

Decline of church membership in relation to population growth 1975-1985 in Britain

FIG. 1a

18.6

16.9

15.3

Most of the major denominations – Anglican, Roman Catholic, Methodist, Presbyterian – reported a decline in membership during 1985. Of those denominations with over 100,000 members only the Baptist, Orthodox and Independent churches (mainly the house churches) reported any growth. These figures for church membership are depressing enough, but statistics from the same source show that in some churches as few as 60% of these members attend church regularly.

REASONS FOR DECLINE

Why is there such a decline in Christianity in this country, even though the church worldwide is growing? Any attempt to answer this question here will fail to do justice to the complexities of the subject. However, I will highlight three major factors that I have observed making a distinctive contribution to this decline.

A GROWTH IN MATERIALISM

We live in a consumer society. As I write these words the trend in this country is towards spending rather than saving. More and more people regard luxury goods as the norm. Sales of videos, dishwashers and compact disc players continue to increase. It seems that people are so engrossed in material goods that spiritual matters are left on the sideline.

RELIGION IS PUSHED TO THE SIDELINES

The growth of materialism is closely linked to the process of secularization. Historically, the church was one of the most powerful institutions in this country. Now its influence is very low. Apart from any other factor, people's increased mobility has made it very difficult for the local church to maintain the influence it once had.

Not only have religious institutions been marginalized, but religious ideas have become less meaningful. My generation (late 50's baby boom) is under the impression that science conflicts with religious belief. Science has unquestionably won the battle. Today's young people grow up in a society where religion is outmoded; their parents would be very unlikely to have any church background. All of our needs can be met by technology, so why should there be any need for a God?

THE PRIVATE NATURE OF BELIEF

Religion has become a taboo subject. People prefer any beliefs they may have to remain a purely private matter. This leads to a proliferation of homegrown philosophies and religious beliefs. It also gives rise to the attitude, 'It doesn't matter what you believe'; everyone is entitled to believe whatever he or she likes. This is not surprising in a society which has been heavily influenced by existentialist philosophies.

Another result is religious pluralism – all religions are seen as valid, so none can claim to be the only true way. The exclusive claims of Christianity are watered down, and spiritual interest is diverted to faiths other than traditional, biblical Christianity. It is alarming to see that any vestige of curiosity in religion is so often channelled into other faiths, cults and the occult. Christians must take their share of the responsibility for this, since the facts show that people are under the impression that Christianity cannot meet their needs. In many school classroom situations Christianity evokes a response of apathy or at worst hostility; any mention of the paranormal, however, quickly arouses interest.

In December 1986 a survey[3] revealed that 79% of people questioned believed in God. Local church surveys in which I have been involved show that many people consider themselves to be Christians, even though they might not pray, read the Bible or attend church regularly. The idea that God is interested in them as an individual, however, does not figure. They have no awareness of the immediacy of God.

Clearly, something does not add up. The trend in society is towards a marginalization of religion, and yet there is a latent interest in spiritual matters. Man *is* a religious animal. There is an awareness of a spiritual dimension to life in each of us, but the pressures of society often keep it locked away in the subconscious. The church needs to change this situation by making an impact on society at both local and national levels. If we do not, other belief systems will.

While the number of church members in Britain declined by 6.5% in the five years to 1985, adherents to other major religions increased by over 29%. The number of Moslems in this country is growing rapidly, and has already overtaken the combined total of Methodists and Baptists by some 150,000 adherents. Immigration accounts for the strong representation of world religions in Britain but it cannot fully explain their growth. It certainly is not a major factor in the growth of the Jehovah's Witnesses and Mormons. Membership of such cults in Britain increased by 1.2% over the same period. (See figure 1b.)

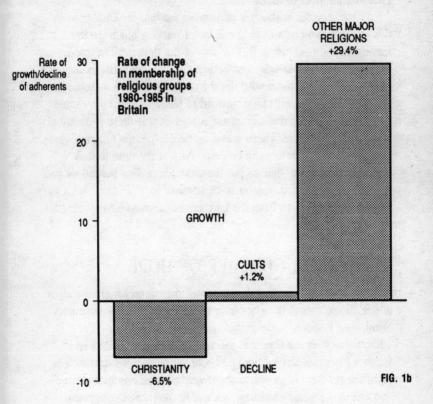

FIG. 1b

If other faiths in Britain can grow then why not Christianity? Perhaps we have lost our appetite for growth. Or perhaps our confidence is low. The idea that the world is against us and that the only thing we can hope for is to maintain our present position insidiously weakens a church's resolve to evangelize. Meanwhile the Jehovah's Witnesses flourish through their evangelistic endeavours. Their number is increasing at a rate of over 2% per annum. Islam is comitted to evangelism; Government statistics estimate that Islam will grow by

21% in Britain between 1985 and 1990[4], if the trend continues to accelerate at the current rate. It is apparent that not only can we learn from the church overseas where Christianity is growing rapidly, but other religions and cults also have much to teach us in terms of their commitment to evangelism.

These statistics make very depressing reading for Christians in this country. No one would blame us for packing our bags and leaving on the next plane! But we should not despair. The good news is that God is on our side, and he is a God who delights in showing us that he can do the impossible. 'Mission: Impossible' becomes 'Mission: Possible' with God. Instead of feeling despair we should be excited. The positive side of the picture is that there is plenty of scope for evangelism! There are many people-groups to reach, and many ways in which this can be done. Now is the time to look outward. Now is the time to put the church's decline behind us and to step out with a firm resolve to be involved in what God wants to do to bring individuals from the kingdom of darkness into his kingdom of light.

A GLIMMER OF HOPE

In small pockets of activity up and down the country there *are* signs of life. Some churches *are* growing numerically. A fellowship in South-east London began with fourteen members in July 1974. By 1987, there were 1600 people meeting in 23 congregations and Ichthus Christian Fellowship had become a household name[5]. The main reason for this growth is the strong emphasis on evangelism that lies at the heart of that church's philosophy. Such spectacular growth is rare in a British church, but modest increases are not so unusual now as they were several years ago. Stopsley Baptist Church in Luton, had a membership of 90 in 1978. Within ten years that had increased to 210. My own church of Christ Church in Welwyn Garden City has seen an equivalent increase over the same length of time. Population movements account for some of the new membership. Many members have moved into the town. But equally, many move away. Alongside the migratory pattern, there has been a steady stream of conversions.

Invariably, lively fellowships such as these three will attract Christians from other churches, but at the same time a significant proportion of this growth is the result of conversions.

Some churches only know growth – decline has never featured in their history. These are mainly the house churches, whose history is admittedly short. But if it can happen in certain parts of the church it can happen in others.

We still have a long way to go. Even the relatively successful churches are only scratching the surface. But these examples show us that there *is* hope. Numerical growth *can* occur. Lessons *can* be learnt.

THE NEED FOR REVIVAL

Numerical growth is closely linked with spiritual revival. The Concise Oxford Dictionary defines revival as a 'reawakening of religious fervour'. In essence the spiritual temperature increases! Revival is a supernatural work of God which leads to a greater depth of commitment among his followers and to an increase in their numbers. We can work towards and pray towards revival, but whether or not it occurs is in the sovereign will of God.

Does this make us redundant? The answer is an emphatic No! Regardless of whether or not revival actually occurs we should still be working towards the same end. God expects our obedience in this. He is gracious, and so he allows us to play a part in a process that often leads to revival. God chooses to work in partnership with his church. Just as he worked through Jesus when he lived in Palestine 2000 years ago, so he now works through Jesus' 'body' on earth – the church.

We know that the decline in the number of church members in Britain contradicts God's desires. He 'wants all men to be saved and to come to a knowledge of the truth' (1 Timothy 2:4). God longs for everyone to enter into a personal relationship with him, through believing in Christ. He wants to see his church grow; he wants to see individuals coming into his family, experiencing the warmth of his love, joy and peace. Through his Spirit God is seeking to bring life to his church.

THE KEY TO REVIVAL

The Yoida Full Gospel Church of Seoul, Korea, had 500,000 members in 1987. This is not a denomination, it is a single church. In fact it is the largest church in the world. In 1982, 110,000 Koreans became Christians through the ministry of this church – only 60,000 were absorbed into membership, the remaining 50,000 joined other churches. In 1984, the church was growing at a rate of 12,000 members a month.[6]

The pastor, Dr Paul Yonggi Cho started his ministry in this church when it met in a marquee. His book, *Prayer: the Key to Revival* sums up the central and vital role of prayer in the growth of that church. Cho himself rises at 5 a.m. each day to spend time in prayer. The church owns land on a hillside known as 'Prayer Mountain' where thousands of Korean Christians go to pray each year. Prayer is given top priorty.

The phenomenal growth of this church can be attributed to a number of factors, including sociological ones that are unique to Korea, but none of these can detract from the central role of prayer. And Cho writes 'It has been historically true that prayer has been the key to every revival in the history of Christianity'.[7]

DISCOVERING GOD'S PLANS

In our partnership with God, he is the senior partner, the managing director and chief executive all rolled into one. We are aware of God's general desire, but what about the details? Does God have plans for them? Can we discover God's plans? We don't need to look further than the example of Jesus to answer this question. Jesus spent hours in prayer. He sought his Father's will throughout his ministry. We see him praying before choosing the twelve, before the crucifixion, and when ministering to individuals. How much more necessary is it for us to seek God's heart and mind when making plans to introduce others to him? We need to ensure that we really work in partnership with him, rather than press on with our man-made schemes. Our own ideas may seem good, but if God is not in them, they will not achieve anything more than short-lived, hollow success. We therefore need to discover God's plans. This is the first stage in our prayer for revival.

PRAYER

The sort of prayer where we seek to discern God's will and make our decisions accordingly has been called 'board room prayer'. The next stage is to pray for the activities that result, and for the people God wants to bring into his kingdom.

In the early church, the disciples spent the time leading up to the Pentecost feast in prayer. As they prayed, God was preparing to reveal his power through the Holy Spirit. When this actually happened, 3000 people were added to their number. In the 18th century, Ludwig von Zinzendorf established a Christian community which initially struggled. In despair, Zinzendorf turned to God in prayer. He instituted a Prayer Watch with people praying night and day. It lasted for over a hundred years. Not only did the community experience renewal, but there was also a zeal for mission. 2000 missionaries travelled to Europe and the rest of the world, preaching the good news of Jesus Christ, and caring for the sick and the poor.[8]

These incidents, one from the early church, the other from later church history, are just two examples among many of the same principle at work. In both, the main prayer emphasis was to discern the mind of God. People tuned into God's wavelength to discover his concerns and his will.

EXTRAORDINARY PRAYER

Two further examples show the power of prayer in outreach. They are both examples of 'extraordinary prayer' – the prayer of ordinary people expecting a response from an extraordinary God. Such prayer is being encouraged by Youth For Chirst worldwide.

Kwee Siew works in the YFC office in Singapore. She has become the dynamo in encouraging prayer for revival. In 1986, as a result of her work, 300 young Christians committed themselves to praying for non-Christian friends; over 100 young people have become Christians as a result of God answering those prayers.[8]

Closer to home, in Epping Forest, fifteen youngsters formed themselves into 'A-Teams' to pray for friends in the six weeks leading up to a mission event in 1987. As a result, five of these friends made a commitment to follow Christ. This in itself is not revival, but it does show what can happen. If every fifteen Christians in the country prayed in this way and the same results occurred: that would be a revival experience.

Revival is the release of the power of God bringing life to people who are spiritually dead. Yet without prayer there will more often than not be no release of this power. Prayer precedes revival; prayer underlines and strengthens revival; prayer is encouraged by revival.

THE PROBLEM WITH PRAYER

British Youth For Christ worker Mike Morris was involved in training a group of young Christians who were about to embark on a volunteer team project. He asked the group what were the most important things that should be encouraged in the lives of new Christians. Several replies were given, but at the top of the list were prayer and reading the Bible. Later in the seminar, Mike asked what areas of the Christian life did the team members find most difficult. They replied: prayer and reading the Bible.

This summarizes the dilemma. Prayer is central to the Christian life. It is one of the foundation stones, and yet it is something with which most Christians have difficulties. Even 'professional' Christians, such as ministers, evangelists and others in full-time Christian service, the ones who are put on pedestals by fellow-Christians, find difficulty in keeping their prayer life alive. But despite this being a common problem, we *can* do something to change the situation.

TOWARDS A SOLUTION

What can we do to improve the quality of our relationship with God?

1. The first stage is to **recognize the problem**. It's no use fooling ourselves by pretending that everything is fine when our relationship with God is suffering because we don't spend the time talking with him in prayer. Honesty is beneficial.

2. The second step is to **admit our failure**. If we confess our

failure, God will forgive us (see 1 John 1:8, 9), and he can then begin to work in us again.

3. We are then in a position to **pinpoint negative factors** that hinder our praying. This may include things like lack of time, wandering thoughts, lack of stamina, lack of fellowship. It may be a specific problem which is sapping our energy.

4. When we have put our finger on the things that are hindering us, we will be in a position to **replace the negative with the positive**. If we lack the time to pray, for example, we may decide to replace one activity that takes up our time with prayer, or make the time available during our lunch-break, or put into the diary a priority appointment for prayer, say an hour or two each week. We may seek a prayer partner. We may need to seek the counsel of an older Christian.

We need to use our common sense, our imagination and our courage to give ourselves greater opportunity to pray. The action sheet at the end of this chapter develops this approach.

PRAYING TOGETHER

I have heard the church prayer meeting called the powerhouse of the church. This used to puzzle me. For one thing, some churches do not meet to pray in this way. For another it does not reflect my experience of prayer meetings, and I suspect there are many others with similar experiences. Often the meetings lack any signs of life; the same people pray the same prayer week after week; there are long embarrassed silences; attendance is pitiful. It is often the meeting that most people avoid! The most alarming aspect is that the church prayer meeting very often reflects the personal prayer life of the people who attend!

Again, variety and a sense of vibrancy and expectancy need to be brought into our corporate praying. Prayer concerts are one way of achieving this. The term was used by the eighteenth-century evangelist, Jonathan Edwards, but more recently has come into prominence in the World-wide Youth Prayer Movement pioneered by Youth For Christ International. The idea is to use several different forms of praying in the same evening – silent prayer, individual prayer, small and large groups, spontaneous praying, prepared praying, simultaneous praying out loud, different postures for prayer, etc. Not only is it enjoyable – it can bear some relationship to party-type games, although it is not frivolous – but it also means that far more praying can be done in a concerted manner. These ideas are expanded and included with many others in *Prayer Pacesetting* by John Earwicker.[8] Although the book is aimed at youth groups, churches are beginning to adopt some of the concepts and methods for a wider age range, and now find them to be an invaluable resource.

PERSEVERANCE IN PRAYER

But sometimes we feel that praying is the last thing we want to do. We know there is a problem, but nothing seems to work; there is no breakthrough in sight. Unfortunately there is no easy answer to this: prayer can be hard work. Even David who wrote so many inspiring Psalms sometimes found it hard to pray. He had to will himself to do it, even though he did not want to.

Prayer, when everything is said and done, is a matter of the will, not of whether or not we feel like praying. So even when we don't feel that we are 'getting through', we have to trust in the fact that God desires that we commune with him in prayer. He longs for us to spend time with him. *Prayer is about our relationship with God.* God longs for us to have a *good* relationship with him. Therefore he will honour our intentions, even though we may feel nothing at the time. It is a matter of the will, and it is a matter of faith. God promises to hear our prayers. God *will* answer them, and where they are in line with his will, he acts on them.

Above all, we need to change our attitude to prayer. Prayer is an adventure: a very rewarding adventure. Therefore we must persevere through the dry patches so that during the good times we take every advantage of, and encouragement from, the excitement of experiencing the presence of God in prayer and seeing him answer our requests.

FROM PRAYER TO ACTION

Jesus was moved by compassion when he saw crowds of people going in and out of the towns and villages. He likened them to sheep without a shepherd. Recognizing that prayer was the key to their salvation he instructed his followers to 'ask the Lord of the harvest ... to send out workers into his harvest field' (Matthew 9:38). This is the last verse of a chapter, and normally people would stop reading at that point. However, if they continued into the next chapter they would discover that the prayer was answered. Workers did go out into the harvest field taking the good news of Jesus Christ. Who were those workers? None other than the disciples who had been involved in the praying. Prayer is vital to revival, but as the disciples discovered it is inseparably linked with action.

God chooses to work through his people. Therefore, when we ask God to act in any particular situation, he will normally do so through his church – in other words you and me. Our part is not only to talk to God about the situation, but to listen to him as he reveals his plans and then to put them into action. We know that God wants all people to be saved, so we can expect to be involved in the process of taking the means of their salvation to them. We are to be bearers of the good news. The main purpose of this book is to help churches to do this in the last few years of the twentieth century.

Christ's command to 'go and make disciples' demands a response on our part. When we have prayed, and have been convicted of the need for action, the question remains, what kind of action? For many, the answer that first comes to mind might be 'Let's organize a mission'. However, this solution can do more harm than good, unless we are wary. Indeed, missions are potentially very dangerous to the outreach of the church.

BEWARE – MISSIONS!

There are three main dangers that need to be recognized. They recur time and time again, and are usually in evidence in many situations where missions fail to achieve much of lasting value. We need to be aware of them so that we can take the necessary precautions either to avoid them altogether, or to minimize their harmful results.

1. OVER-DEPENDENCE ON PERSONALITIES

Whenever the idea of organizing a church mission is raised, it is never long before the question of 'Who shall we ask to lead the outreach?' arises. Immediately we have walked into a minefield! There are three particular danger areas:

'That lets me out!'

'Now the experts are coming,' thinks many a church member, 'there is no need for me to get involved.' After all, the professionals are getting paid to do the evangelism, and they have the necessary experience. This pattern does not conform to the biblical example of 'every member involvement' in the church. It is a theme to which I shall return in due course.

Who will follow up?

Even if the church uses an outside evangelist or an evangelistic team, the follow-up of new Christians, or those who have expressed an interest, is still the task of the church. If church members have left the evangelism entirely to the team, however, there will be a very tenuous link between themselves and those who were contacted in the mission. Follow-up is made very difficult.

I am suspicious of any claim by evangelistic teams that tens of thousands have been converted through their ministry. Such claims are certainly not reflected in the figures for church attendance or membership. Where are all the converts now? If they did make a genuine commitment there seems to be a problem in the follow-up.

The messenger or the message?

There is an inherent problem in using gifted evangelists, musicians or other prominent personalities, and that is that people will sometimes respond to them rather than to their message. This is especially true of singers and bands involved in youth evangelism.

I firmly believe that there is a place for itinerant evangelists and teams, and that they have gifts and abilities that are especially useful in mission activity. However, all three of these problem areas need to be taken into account.

2. OVER-DEPENDENCE ON ACTIVITY

Evangelistic missions are very time consuming, and the sense of busyness can be overwhelming. Whenever a period of mission comes to an end we are always 'in need of a holiday'. But this intense activity can be very misleading. It can give the impression that we must have achieved a lot. When we come to look at the results in broad daylight, this is often very far from the truth. We need to be aware of the ratio between effort and achievement, and to concentrate on those types of evangelism where the results bear a closer relationship to the effort put in.

This problem is most dangerous when we concentrate so much on organizing the evangelistic activity that the actual evangelism suffers. 'We didn't see many outsiders reached, but the church has grown much closer together' is a sad indictment on any evangelistic activity. There are other ways of improving our fellowship; the main aim of evangelism must always be to bring people into the kingdom of God.

3. OVER-DEPENDENCE ON THE EVENT

The third danger is of putting all our eggs into one basket. We do our evangelistic 'bit' for the year and then collapse into a heap until next time. Inviting friends along to activities and sharing our faith with them is shelved until that special time of the year occurs. But outreach should never be restricted to missions. It's an all-round-the-year activity. A mission event should always be seen as part of the continual outreach of the church. If we ever see it as anything else then we have not understood the real meaning of mission, which goes far beyond the idea of a special activity.

These three dangers warn us that some forethought is necessary before planning a mission or programme of evangelism. We need to discover the pattern that God has given us in his word. It is to that pattern that we will now turn.

BIBLICAL MISSION: WHAT IS IT?

Jesus' Great Commission to his followers, quoted at the beginning of this chapter, is a command: 'Go and make disciples. . .'. Jesus does not explain how this is to be done until immediately before the ascension. In the record of Acts 1, there are two very important principles concerning the 'how' of evangelism. Both are found in verse 8: 'But you will receive power when the Holy Spirit comes on you; and you will be my witnesses . . . to the ends of the earth.'

The first principle is the need for God's power. This comes in the form of the Holy Spirit. Without the Holy Spirit we can forget about any ideas of bringing people into God's kingdom. The Spirit gives us the courage to share our faith and the words to use. Furthermore, it is the work of the Holy Spirit to convict people of their sin, and to convince them of their need for Christ. The Holy Spirit is central to evangelism.

The second principle is that we are to be witnesses to Jesus throughout the earth. Jesus does not say you ought to be, but you *will* be! It was this day-to-day, personal witness that formed the undercurrent to the rapid expansion of the early church. Peter, Paul and Stephen may have grabbed the headlines with their preaching, but it was against the background of the believers spreading the good news by word of mouth, from house to house. This activity underlines the central theme of Paul's thinking on the church, that every member has a part to play. We are *all* called to be witnesses.

The same idea features in the Old Testament. God declares to his people: 'You are my witnesses' (Isaiah 43:10,12). This is still true today. The writer of Psalm 66 says, 'Let me tell you what he has done for me' (verse 16), and Isaiah likewise, 'I will tell of the kindnesses of the Lord, the deeds for which he is to be praised' (Isaiah 63:7). This urge to tell others is evident in the early church – Peter and John declared, 'We cannot help speaking about what we have seen and heard' (Acts 4:20).

The instructions to early Christians apply to us, too. Peter writes, 'Always be prepared to give an answer to everyone who asks you to give a reason for the hope that you have' (1 Peter 3:15). Paul exhorts us: 'Do not be ashamed to testify about our Lord' (2 Timothy 1:8).

Only some people are gifted as natural evangelists and called to make evangelism their main task, but there is no biblical restriction on who should be a witness. It is an obligation for all Christ's followers. Our mission is *'to boldly go'!*

| NOTES |

1. This is a gross oversimplification of the facts. Christianity reached Africa and Asia during the centuries immediately following Christ's death. However it did not penetrate these continents to any great degree until the European Expansion from the 16th century onwards.

2. These figures, and those following, are taken from the *UK Christian Handbook* 1989/90 (MARC Europe/Evangelical Alliance/Bible Societies).

3. From a Marplan Poll published in *Sunday Express*, 7 December 1986.

4. *Social Trends 18*, Central Statistical Office, 1988

Myrtle Langley in her book *Religions* (Lion Publishing), comments that Islam 'is a militantly missionary religion . . . set to conquer the world'. This evangelistic fervour is difficult to separate from the militancy of certain Islamic sects, particularly the fundamentalists. As Christians we need to realize that a Moslem is a person loved by God, and for whom Jesus died. Our response to Moslems should not be one of fear but of love and concern. We should seek to win them for Christ through love, not counter-attack.

5. Unfortunately there is no accurate way of knowing how much of this growth is directly attributable to conversions. Ichthus have not carried out a survey of their membership since early in their history, when the rate of growth was higher than it is now. At that time, approximately half of new members were converted through the work of the fellowship. A spokesman from Ichthus estimates that currently this figure would be between 20 and 30 per cent, although this is only an informed guess.

6. Information extrapolated from:
Prayer: Key to Revival, Paul Y Cho and R. Whitney Manzano (Word Books, 1985)
More than Numbers, Paul Y Cho (Word, 1987)
Operation World 4th Edition, Ed.

Patrick Johnstone (STL/WEC, 1986), esp. p269

7. *Prayer: Key to Revival* p7

8. *Prayer Pacesetting*, John Earwicker (Scripture Union, 1987)

| SUMMARY |

- The church in Britain is declining in membership. This contrasts with
  □ the church worldwide,
  □ other religions and cults in Britain.
- The church needs revival. This is God's desire.
- Prayer is vital for revival:
  □ to discern God's plan,
  □ to intercede for evangelistic activities and people to be reached.

- Mission activity is a natural outworking of prayer.
- Dangers in missions include over-dependence on:
  □ personalities,
  □ activity,
  □ the event itself.
- The biblical view of mission stresses the role of every Christian as a witness.

| ACTION SHEET 1 |

This action sheet will provide valuable background work for Chapter 2. Before using the action sheets, please read the Introduction (p8).

SESSION A

EXERCISE 1
BEFORE THE SESSION – Arrange for someone to look back over church records for the last five years, and gather information about comings and goings from the church fellowship. Have numbers grown or declined during this time? Why have people joined the fellowship? Have they moved into the area? Have they moved from another church? Are they from a non-church background?

15 MINUTES – Present your findings to the whole group. Divide into groups of four or five, and spend fifteen minutes discussing the figures. Account for the changes, or

lack of change, in the size of the church fellowship. What do you conclude about the outreach of the church?

10 MINUTES – Report your conclusions to the whole group.

EXERCISE 2
10 MINUTES – In the same groups, consider your church's teaching programme over the last couple of years. Preaching plans and house group programmes should be at hand. Has there been enough encouragement for witnessing? Has there been practical training? Has it been effective?

10 MINUTES – Now look to the future. Suggest ways in which your preaching/teaching programme could include the following elements:
  □ encouragement to witness,
  □ teaching on how to witness (Is this teaching practical?),
  □ opportunities for people to talk about their faith in a real and natural way,
  □ opportunities for people to 'give their testimony' – ie say in public what God has been doing in their life,
  (These last two will help people to 'practise' sharing their faith),
  □ opportunity and encouragement for members to pray for one another about specific witnessing opportunities.

5 MINUTES – Report back to the whole group.

EXERCISE 3 ACTION EXTRA
5 MINUTES – INTRODUCTION – Ask group members to keep a record of how they spend their time between now and the next meeting (at least one week). It is important to record how long they spend on each activity – eating, sleeping, working, attending meetings, hobbies, watching TV, time with family, etc.

SESSION B

EXERCISE 4
10 MINUTES –
  □ Give each group member a sheet of paper as in figure 1c. Individually, members write down everyone they can think of who falls into each of the categories.
  □ Underline all those who are not yet Christian.
The result is your church's most promising mission-field!

5 MINUTES –
  □ Add up the total numbers for the whole group.
  □ Each member picks out the names of three people for whom

PEOPLE I KNOW

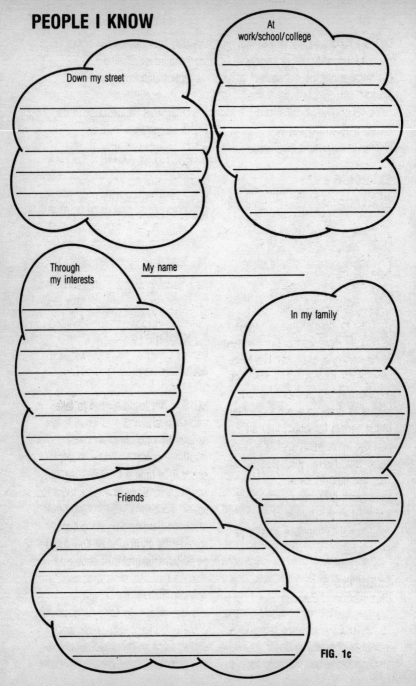

At work/school/college

Down my street

Through my interests

My name

In my family

Friends

FIG. 1c

they have a particular concern or with whom they have a special relationship.
□ Form into groups of three.
□ Each person takes two minutes to tell the others about the three people they have picked out.

10 MINUTES – In threes, spend the next 10 minutes praying for these people, and for God's help in witnessing to them. Each triplet will have prayed for nine non-Christians by the end of this exercise.

You can suggest that people continue to meet in triplets in order to pray for their friends. For the sake of convenience, they may like to re-arrange the triplets if they are to be more permanent. It may help the triplets to draw up a prayer profile of the people for whom they are praying. Information should include name, age, family, job, hobbies, etc. This will help those who do not know them personally to be more informed in their praying. No confidential information should be recorded.

EXERCISE 5
(Resumption of Exercise 3 in Session A)
15 MINUTES – In pairs discuss the timetable of how you spent your time since the last meeting. Are you satisfied with the way in which you used the time?

How much time was spent:
□ in meetings?
□ in front of the TV?
□ intimately with God?
□ invested in other people, especially non-Christians?
Notice how much time Jesus invested in people. (We'll be looking at this in chapter 2.) What can you do to improve?

10 MINUTES – Ask people to share their findings and any suggestions they might have to make better use of their time with the whole group. Is there anything that the church leaders could do to help members use their time more profitably?

NOTE – The leaders need to take this seriously, and it is good to get people thinking about it before reading chapter 2. Where people spend little time with non-Christians, what can be done to enable them to spend more time? (Eg cutting down meetings; joining interest groups outside the church, etc.) You could get together a group of people to discuss this. Brainstorming could be very productive. This means allowing people to say any ideas that come into their head. These are immediately written down, and no-one is allowed to comment on them until you finish 'storming, and begin to sift through the ideas.

Now that you have some idea of the problem you can begin to motivate people to use their time for witnessing. You will also need to think about where people spend much time with non-Christians but with little effect. What can be done to maximize their witnessing opportunities?

EXERCISE 6 ACTION EXTRA

5 MINUTES – INTRODUCTION – ask group members to consider their prayer life before the next meeting. Are they satisfied with their personal prayer times? Are there any areas that can be improved? They should use the following table to list areas of concern. Against each area note the negative and positive factors that affect each one, and after due consideration, decide how to tackle the issue. The example shown below will help.

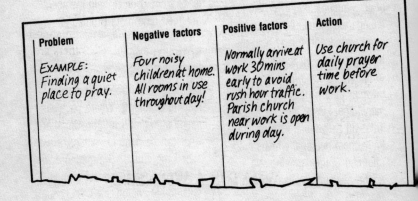

Problem	Negative factors	Positive factors	Action
EXAMPLE: Finding a quiet place to pray.	Four noisy children at home. All rooms in use throughout day!	Normally arrive at work 30 mins early to avoid rush hour traffic. Parish church near work is open during day.	Use church for daily prayer time before work.

'YOU SHALL BE MY WITNESSES'

THE IMPORTANCE OF PERSONAL WITNESS

Before we think about evangelistic activities and missions, we need to ensure that there is a basis of continuous personal witness on which to build. Without it our hopes for church growth may never be realized.

'Witnessing' is a very misunderstood term. Some Christians only use it to describe open-air evangelism or street evangelism, eg approaching people on the streets to offer them leaflets about Christianity, or to share the gospel with them (sometimes in a most intrusive and objectionable manner, although thankfully others are more sensitive). Others use it to describe conversations with total strangers in railway carriages, which invariably end in their taking a copy of a gospel, and praying a prayer of commitment – or at least that is the impression we are given. Both definitions are much too narrow.

WHAT IS A WITNESS?

Two helpful illustrations of 'being a witness' show that witnessing to Jesus is within the grasp of *all* Christians.

The first illustration is the role of a witness in a court of law. A witness relates to the court what he or she has seen, heard and experienced, in relation to the crime that is under investigation. The police will have appealed for witnesses, so that they can discover what has actually occurred in that particular incident. In the same way, a witness to Christ is someone who relates all that he has seen, heard and experienced of Jesus in his life.

The second illustration of a 'witness' derives from advertising. The aim of an advertisement is to persuade the consumer to buy a particular product. A good advertisement makes an impact and sticks in our minds, acting as a reminder of the product it is trying to sell. It must not make false claims; it must be a true 'witness' to the product. Millions of people still remember the clever PG Tips commercials in which chimps were dressed up, and human voices dubbed in. More recently, advertisements for shares in British Gas captured the imagination of the public as 'Sid' became a national institution. It was impossible to get away from references to him. He even made headlines in national papers!

As Christians we need to be advertisements for Jesus, constantly bringing him to the minds of the people we meet.

A good Christian witness, then, is one who through his words and his lifestyle introduces people to the living Lord Jesus Christ. The way we live, the way we react in tricky situations, speaks volumes. 'Actions speak louder than words.' Because actions stem from attitudes, it is also a question of what we are. In order to be a good witness, we need to grow more like Jesus in our attitudes and behaviour. But this is easier said than done!

TO BE OR NOT TO BE?

There is a paradox in the Christian life. On the one hand all those who repent and believe in Christ are seen as guiltless before God. This is made possible by Jesus' death on the cross. On the other hand, we all know that we carry on living imperfect lives; we can never hope to live as Christ lived: without sin.

The Bible is clear that it is our duty to aim for perfection by modelling our lives on Jesus, and our inability to match God's standards must not deter us from our efforts. Other Christians whose lives reflect his character are also good models: an example to follow is always helpful.

The danger with setting very high standards and ideals for ourselves, however, is that we can become very discouraged when we fail to live up to them. This can lead to self-condemnation and guilt. It is far more helpful to compare our lives now with how they were before we became Christians. Inevitably there will have been changes for the better, because God promises that this will be so. We may find that we are able to resist some temptations where once we would have given in; we may find ourselves able to build relationships with people that we used to find impossible. We will certainly not be perfect, but we will have improved. It is this improvement that witnesses to others.

The Christian life is not easy, and effort is involved, but God helps us to become more like Jesus. As we grow in our personal relationship with God, and so realize the constant need to change, so God's Spirit is at work in us, supernaturally changing our attitudes. Sometimes other people will perceive a difference in our lives when we are least aware of it. This shows God's goodness to us.

We can now see that training events on 'How to witness' can be misleading if they concentrate almost exclusively on how to tell others the good news. How we live is just as important, if not more so, than what we say. We need to be aware of both aspects in our witnessing.

The beauty of witnessing is the fact that it is a natural outworking of our Christian commitment. Thus, above everything else, a witness is someone who loves Jesus. The challenge to us is clear: it is a challenge full of hope – do you love Jesus? Our love for him can only be a response to his tremendous love for us. Will you let that love affect every area of your life? Unfortunately, we are in danger of falling into the trap of legalism whereby witnessing becomes a list of do's and don't's. If we concentrate on loving Jesus I am sure that our efforts to please him in what we do will be the best witness that we can offer.

ALL CHRISTIANS ARE WITNESSES

Evangelism must always include the personal witness of believers; it must always take place against the background of constant witnessing if it is to be fully effective. The moment evangelism is divorced from day-to-day, personal witness it will flounder. There may well be spectacular incidents, such as vast numbers committing their lives to following Christ at an event, but unless there is a constant witness in the background, the vast numbers can just as easily dwindle.

Over the years I have been involved in several missions based in secondary schools. At the end we would invariably hold an evangelistic concert off the school premises. At one such concert, fifty young people responded to the challenge to commit their lives to Christ. At another about twenty-five responded. In both cases, within a matter of a few days those same youngsters wanted nothing to do with a Christian commitment. Those teenagers in the schools who have become Christians, and are now growing in the faith, have generally done so as a result of the witness of their friends. It was the support and witness of those involved in a school Christian Union and church youth group that helped Claire to grow in her faith. For Alistair it was the witness of a Christian friend that proved to be the decisive factor. These are the successes in my work, not the spectacular flash-in-the-pan phenomena that soon fizzle out. Concerts and similar events do have an important part to play but this should always be in conjunction with individual evangelism through relationships. The real successes bear testimony to the effectiveness of this personal witness.

It is through the witness of Christians that people will see the reality of the gospel, and through the same witness they will be encouraged in their growth as new Christians. This is the outworking of Paul's injunction: 'Follow my example, as I follow the example of Christ' (1 Corinthians 11:1). A life changed by the power and love of Christ is one of the most convincing arguments for the Christian faith.

SOME ARE EVANGELISTS

We are not all called by God to be evangelists. An evangelist specializes in proclaiming the gospel, bringing people to Christ, and he or she will often motivate others to witness. Sometimes this involves speaking at evangelistic events, sometimes making contact with individuals and sharing the gospel with them in the street, in their homes or at their place of work. This is a ministry given by God to specific Christians, and it is their main area of responsibility in the Church. However, *all* Christians are called to be witnesses, and since witnessing is an integral part of evangelism, we are all called to be *involved* in evangelism. Evangelism should be the business of every member of the church.

The effectiveness of our evangelism will improve as more Christians play an active role through personal witness to their friends and contacts.

IMPROVING OUR WITNESS

If your reaction to the previous section is 'I've never really thought about it in this way before', then it is clear that we need to be educated. If your reaction is 'Well, I realize all this, but have never really done anything about it', then we need to put what we know into practice. In either case, the first stage in improving our witness will be motivation.

MOTIVATED TO WITNESS

In the light of Christ's final command to his disciples to 'go and make disciples' it seems scandalous that outreach is not a motivating force in the lives of so many Christians. Far from it, the idea of personally being involved in bringing people to recognize Jesus Christ as their Lord and Saviour, except as a distant observer, often does not even enter their heads. Motivation can be achieved in various ways, including the following:

PERSONAL EXAMPLE
The most important way of motivating others to witness, and probably the most effective, is through personal example. If we want people to do something then we need to show them how. This may mean that we then become a model for them, but more likely we are simply an inspiration. If they see something achieved by our witnessing, others will be fired with enthusiasm. It will seem within their grasp. If they can be convinced that witnessing is not the prerogative solely of the 'super-saints', half the battle is won.

The reverse is also true. People cannot do things if they have no pattern to follow. This is a challenge to those in a leadership position: we should be giving that example. Certainly this is the case in witnessing. It's no good expecting others to witness if we are not prepared to make any effort ourselves. This will be particularly poignant if you are a 'professional' Christian – someone involved in so-called 'full-time ministry'. It is very easy to find yourself coming into less and less contact with non-Christians, let alone having any as friends. Being a minister or a vicar is not a let-out from personal witnessing, so time and energy needs to be invested in building friendships.

PREACHING AND TEACHING

Preaching inspires us to act, and teaching shows us how. Church life provides plenty of opportunities to motivate church members to witness. We must be careful, though, not merely to harangue the congregation each time we have them in our grip, or to make the members of the house group feel guilty each time they meet. Instead, we must show that witnessing is within everyone's capability.

There are many ways of teaching. Those in which people take an active part – in discussion, role-play, exercises, simulation games, etc. – are better than just listening. There is some excellent material available that can be adapted to suit your own situation. Scripture Union produced *Care to Say Something?* for Billy Graham's 'Mission England'. The book was designed for groups to use over six sessions, involved a variety of teaching methods, and encouraged participants to put into practice what they learnt. *Person to Person* is the development of this, using interactive video as the basis of the course. This award-winning video training course comprises five 2-hour and five 45-minute sessions. Jim Smith's *Operation Breakthrough* material is in a similar mould although aimed at young people. Further details of all these will be found in the Resources List (Appendix 3). In the meantime, the action sheets will give a flavour of some of the activities used by these courses.

SMALL GROUP SUPPORT

Small group meetings, such as house groups, have a very important role to play in motivation. They are an ideal way to encourage members and monitor their progress as they share their experiences and feelings. They also provide support as members seek to witness, helping them to cope with success and failure. This need for support must not be underestimated: members can learn to recognize and appreciate each other's vulnerability.

Christians need constant motivation. Our human nature insists on it. It is pointless to have an annual sermon on the importance of being a good witness in isolation from anything else. If we want people to see personal witness as an integral part of church life, it needs to be constantly referred to and encouraged throughout the year, with every now and then a special 'push' – perhaps with one of the helps already mentioned. Sermons, for example, could be accompanied by practical teaching in housegroups, using one of the recommended courses.

Motivation requires enthusiasm. There will be a vastly different reaction to the idea of witnessing if leaders are enthusiastic and encouraging than if it is presented merely as our duty. A positive attitude and example will result in a positive reaction.

MOBILIZED TO WITNESS

If our congregation, or group, is fired up and raring to go, then we must ensure that they are given adequate opportunities to put into practice what they have learnt. In this we can give a lead.

PRAYER TRIPLETS

Prayer is vital if our witnessing is to be effective. The idea of meeting in threes to pray for each other in our daily witness is a way of mobilizing people, and God always seems to answer our prayers to create opportunities for witnessing. Meeting together regularly will encourage us to take advantage of those opportunities as the other members of the triplet check on our progress. Prayer triplets were first used in the 1984 'Mission England'. Three group members each list three friends or acquaintances who are not yet Christians, and together the triplet prays for them and for opportunities to lead them to Christ. It is amazing how much has happened through prayer triplets up and down the country over the last few years.[1]

COURSE HOMEWORK

Starting to get into the habit of sharing our faith with others is often the most difficult step. The idea of a little practical 'homework' can be very productive. Setting tasks that people can do to put into practice what they have learnt is an important part of the learning process. Teaching without application will be wasted.

After a session on telling the story of how we came to faith in Christ, for example, the course homework might be to find a non-Christian friend who will help by listening to your story to see if it makes sense. We should take notice of their comments, since we need to learn, but the bonus factor is that in the process we have witnessed to them: they have heard about what God has done in our lives – a testimony to his love and power!

BRIDGE-BUILDING

Too often, the church is its own worst enemy. We say we want to see God's kingdom grow, that we want to bring others to faith in Christ, and yet we thwart this desire at the first hurdle. Church members are often so busy with church activities that they do not have the time to build bridges with the people who most need to hear about Christ. The simple remedy is often unpalatable. The moment we suggest curtailing activities, we find that they have suddenly become very popular, and are seen as being absolutely essential.

If I ever hear anyone say that the church is their whole life, I know that we have failed. God brought the church into being for the sake of the world, not just the benefit of its members. We must be prepared to streamline our weekly programme, and encourage one another to use time productively in building bridges with non-Christian friends. This is the first step towards introducing them to the Lord Jesus Christ.

Once we have cleared this first hurdle, we then encounter the next – our human nature. Witnessing should be second nature to a Christian. If we are honest, though, it is often the one thing most of us would be quite happy to avoid. We much prefer curling up in a cosy armchair to watch the TV, to facing the challenge of sharing our faith with other people. This obstacle, like the first, must be surmounted.

Even when we create the right atmosphere for our churches to be witnessing communities, we may still find that there is a great resistance to making personal evangelism a priority. We need to understand why people are so reluctant to share their faith. The following are some of those reasons.

BUT ...

I'M FRIGHTENED

Is there anyone who has not felt their knees knocking and their stomach churning as an opportunity to say something about their faith has arisen? Perhaps we are unsure of ourselves, or perhaps we think we will be the object of scorn and derision. Whatever the reason, it is a very natural reaction.

The disciples were scared out of their wits after the crucifixion. They remained unsure of themselves even after Jesus had appeared. What changed them was the outpouring of the Holy Spirit at Pentecost. The Spirit gave them a supernatural boldness that took them by surprise. If the disciples needed the Spirit, then how much more do we. Day by day we need to ask to be filled by God with his Spirit of power.

The antidote to fear is love. I myself am naturally terrified of taking part in street evangelism, but I have taken part, and been most encouraged by the support of the other Christians involved. On one particular open-air project I was carried through by the love and the prayers of the others involved, and it was this support that made the difference. Too often the missing component in our evangelism has been that atmosphere of love and caring. The more supportive we are of one another, the more our fear will subside.

I DON'T KNOW WHAT TO SAY

Some Christians feel that they are not clever enough to express their faith. Most of the disciples were uneducated, and yet they became powerful witnesses for Jesus. People could see that they had been with the Lord. We need to spend time with Jesus, and be so full of him that people will be able to tell that there is something different about us, without having to open our mouths. When we do speak, we know that God has promised that the Holy Spirit will give us the right words to say.

We need to allow the Spirit to direct our words and actions. He does this as we read the Bible and put into practice what he teaches. He also does it in a supernatural way, as we submit ourselves to Him and become aware of God's presence and his leading.

I DON'T REALLY KNOW WHAT A WITNESS IS

If we haven't understood what witnessing is, and why it is important, we will flounder. We need to ensure that the teaching and example in our church is clear, and even then we must be prepared to spend time with individuals to make sure they have got the message.

I'M A FAILURE

'How can I be a witness for Jesus? Everything I do goes wrong. I'm no good to anyone, let alone God.' I suspect that is just how Peter felt. Every time he opened his mouth he put both feet in. He denied even knowing Jesus in his hour of need, and then deserted him. Yet Jesus had plans for Peter the Failure, and he became the Rock on which the church was built. The difference was made by an encounter with the risen Lord Jesus and the outpouring of the Holy Spirit. Each person is important in God's eyes, so much so that he was prepared to let Jesus die for us. We need to stress this. It is much harder to say we are failures when we realize just how much God thinks we are worth.

I DON'T GET THE OPPORTUNITY TO SHARE

If we don't *want* an opportunity to share our faith, we can be sure we won't get one! If we want to share our faith with others we need only tell God and he will ensure that the opportunity arises. If you want 'Jesus encounters', ask God for them. Pray for specific opportunities to talk to specific people about him. Very rarely will God let that request go ungranted.

I HAVE NOTHING TO SHARE
We only make this excuse when we are not in a real relationship with God. Perhaps we have never put our trust in him; or perhaps we are far away from God at the time. We need to be in a real relationship with God if we are to share that relationship with others.

We need to deal with these problems if they arise, whether or not they are voiced.

UNITED WE STAND

We are all called to be witnesses and so far I have put emphasis on our *individual* responsibilities. However, there is a very real sense in which the church *as a body* is a witness to the community. Sometimes people are attracted to Christianity by the atmosphere between church members and the way they work together. Our corporate witness is as important as our personal witness: indeed they are complementary.

Witnessing should rarely be a lonely business. If it is, then something is very wrong. In the New Testament, the church is clearly shown to be a corporate body in which there is an interdependence between members. At the very least we should support one another through prayer and encouragement. We should also look for opportunities to witness together, whether informally or through an evangelistic project. There is tremendous strength in working together towards a common goal: something that we would be foolish to ignore.

GEARED UP!

There are a number of other things that we can do to gear our church or group for evangelism through personal witness.

EXPECT!

'Expect nothing and you won't be disappointed' is very true, but often forgotten. If we really want to see our church reaching out into the community by its witness, we need to sow the expectation in the hearts and minds of people. If we want to see our congregation grow in number we must start talking about it so that when it actually happens people will not be surprised. Help people to visualize what the future might hold. Give them a glimpse of other churches, either through reading books, or by visiting a growing church to see what it is like and what kind of atmosphere there is.

HIGHLIGHT ACHIEVEMENTS

When we are involved in a situation it is very hard to see it objectively. Draw people's attention to achievements, even small ones, to encourage them. Sometimes this should be done in personal conversations, sometimes within the context of teaching or preaching. One of the pastors at my own church does it all the time. For example, he might mention how individuals expressed their faith through their actions by their generous offer of accommodation to someone in need. It makes things much more personal, and shows that such achievements are not only important, but are within our grasp.

INVOLVE

Witness is the task of the whole church. We have seen how important it is to motivate the whole church to witness, yet we may miss the mark by making that very point. How? Simply by this. Whenever we think about the 'church's task', we automatically assume that it is the responsibility of *others*. It is vital that we impress on each individual that they are the key.

BE URGENT

We are not just playing a numbers game. We are involved in building God's kingdom here on earth. We often fail to see the whole picture. Christ is going to come back and claim that kingdom as his rightful inheritance. This will not happen until the gospel has been taken to every tribe and nation. We need to catch the vision, and see the urgency of the task. Our witness works towards Christ's return. This is the task he has given to us: *'You shall be my witnesses'!*

THE FINAL WORD

The final word in witnessing must be 'friendship'. Jesus was known as the 'friend of sinners'[2]. He built deep friendships with people – with the twelve, with women followers, and with others. There is an attraction about him as a person and many people were drawn to him. Even in short encounters with individuals we can detect an attempt to build a relationship. This is because Jesus was interested in people. He was even interested in women and children who counted for very little in the society of his day. He was interested in the outcasts of society. Each had value in his eyes.

There is no better example than his. The key to witnessing is friendship; the key to friendship is building a relationship; the key to building a relationship is recognizing the value of each person in God's eyes. The most amazing aspect of Jesus' example is that he invested time in people who would ultimately desert him. He knew this would happen yet he still invested his time in them. This in itself is a witness to the depth of God's love.

We need to ease the pressure of witnessing by just aiming to befriend people – spending time with them, showing a genuine interest in them and in what they are doing, inviting them into our homes, doing things together. As you do this pray for them, and pray that the love of Jesus would overflow from your life. True friends share the good things in their lives. Since Jesus is the best thing in a Christian's life, it is only natural that we should share him as our friendships grow.

I firmly believe that friendship is the most effective style of evangelism, since witnessing occurs in the framework of a relationship. Be a witness for Jesus: be a real friend.

| NOTES |

1. See *Three Times Three Equals Twelve*, Brian Mills (Kingsway, 1986) for an account of the effectiveness of prayer triplets, and how to organize them.

2. Matthew 11:19; Luke 7:34

| SUMMARY |

- Christian witness is fundamental to evangelism.
- A witness is:
  □ someone who tells others what he has seen,
  □ someone who is a good advert for Jesus,
  □ someone who loves Jesus.
- Our words, actions and thoughts are all involved in witnessing. Witnessing is an outworking of our Christian life.
- All Christians are called to be witnesses. Some are called to be evangelists.
- Christians need to be **motivated** to witness through:
  □ the example and inspiration of leaders,
  □ preaching, teaching and small group support,
  □ enthusiasm and encouragement.
- Christians can be **mobilized** to witness by:
  □ taking part in prayer triplets, or similar,
  □ doing tasks which put teaching into practice,
  □ taking the time to build bridges with others,
  □ seeing that witnessing can be a natural part of life.
- To gain momentum in witnessing we should:
  □ implant expectations for growth,
  □ highlight achievements made,
  □ stress the importance of personal involvement,
  □ emphasize the urgency of the task in the light of Christ's return.
- The key to witnessing is friendship.

| ACTION SHEET 2 |

SESSION A

EXERCISE 1

5 MINUTES – Ask group members to report on their individual progress with Action Extra (Exercise 6) from the last session. This needs to be done in an atmosphere of encouragement rather than condemnation towards those who did not manage to complete the exercise so begin by asking for any encouragements that have resulted from putting plans into action. Where people are having problems suggest solutions and pray with them: seek always to encourage.

EXERCISE 2

20 MINUTES – A good witness is someone whose lifestyle speaks volumes! Ask group members to consider their own lives. Ask each person to write down three things they do that please God. If people have problems with this ask their friends to suggest things. It is important to build people up before moving on to the next part.

Which areas of your life do not honour the Lord? Which areas need improving?

☐ in your family relationships,
☐ at work (eg in your business ethics),
☐ in your private life (especially your thoughts and opinions),
☐ in your church life.

As the group listens and considers, read through the ten commandments, the Sermon on the Mount, and/or the practical portions of Paul's letters. Group members should look out for major areas in which they fall short of God's standards.

5 MINUTES – Members list their areas of concern and against each write how they would like to see them improved.

15 MINUTES – Individually, spend some time in silent prayer asking God to give you his supernatural help; and to show you what steps to take. Write these down in a table as on the following page.

EXERCISE 3

10 MINUTES – In groups of three or four, discuss why we find it difficult to talk to others about our faith. Refer to pages 44–46.

10 MINUTES – Discuss how these difficulties can be overcome. Give as many practical ideas as possible, and relate to real-life examples and incidents. Share conclusions with the whole group.

Area of life needing improvement	Target for improvement	Steps to improvement		
		1	2	3
EXAMPLE: Relationship with spouse.	Spend more good quality time together.	Cut down on one weekly meeting. Spend that time with spouse.	Take a holiday together. Leave kids with relations.	Read a good Christian book about marriage together.

SESSION B

EXERCISE 4

10 MINUTES – Ask group to report on any progress as a result of Exercise 2 in Session A of this worksheet. Have any of them put into practice their action plan to improve their prayer life (Exercise 6 in chapter 1)? How are they getting on?

EXERCISE 5

40 MINUTES – This exercise tackles the subject of witnessing to others through conversation. In pairs act out real-life conversations between a Christian and a friend. Each pair should be given a different situation, eg

  □ At work on Monday a colleague asks what you did over the weekend, or,
  □ A friend pops round to see you after having a major row with his/her husband/wife.

Each situation should have potential for saying something to point that person towards Jesus.

After each pair has acted out their conversation, ask the others to comment, first on the good points, and then on what could have been better. Pay special attention to these questions:

□ Is the conversation natural?
□ Is the Christian sensitive towards their partner?
□ Is he/she using language that a non-Christian would understand?

Allow time for people to work on this before showing it to the rest of the group. This should be seen not so much as a rehearsal as an exploration of how conversations progress. In real life we do not have the opportunity to rehearse conversations! The group may prefer to spend most of their time in pairs, rather than having their conversation observed and comments made. In this case the leader should wander around and listen in. If there are examples that would be helpful to bring to the attention of the whole group the leader can ask that pair to run through their conversation in front of the others.

Much of the success of this exercise depends on breaking down people's natural reserve. The leader needs to be sensitive to the mood of the group, and yet firm in encouraging members to take part fully.

PART

2

PREPARATIONS

|CHAPTER|
|T H R E E|

BY ALL MEANS
STYLES AND METHODS OF EVANGELISM

Continuous personal witness is, then, the first and most important
aspect of evangelism and like all our evangelism, it should be built
on a solid foundation of prayer. There is more to evangelism than
witnessing alone, however. In this chapter we will look at the whole
process of evangelism and the activities that can be used in it.

LAYER UPON LAYER

It is helpful to look at these activities in terms of layers, or levels,
that build on one another. This is shown in figure 3a overleaf.

LEVEL 1: PERSONAL WITNESSING
We have looked at this in detail in chapter 2.

LEVEL 2: EVANGELISTIC EMPHASIS
After personal witness, the next layer is an evangelistic emphasis
within the church. This is closely related to personal witness, and it
was referred to in the last chapter. A mission-conscious church will
not restrict its evangelism to special events but will maintain an
evangelistic edge to many of its normal activities. Such an emphasis
heightens our expectations and is often rewarded by a steady trickle
of people committing their lives to Christ. The challenge of the
gospel plays a central part in the programme and preaching of the

LAYERS OF
EVANGELISM

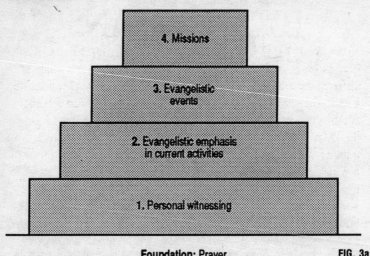

4. Missions

3. Evangelistic events

2. Evangelistic emphasis in current activities

1. Personal witnessing

Foundation: Prayer

FIG. 3a

church, and all those who come into contact with the church will be under no doubts as to its importance.

LEVEL 3: SPECIAL EVENTS
The third layer consists of special events that are evangelistic by design, their whole aim being to reach out to the community and present the Good News of Jesus Christ. Ideally, such events will be part of the church's regular programme of activities, and will form part of an evangelistic strategy. (We look at strategy in chapter 6.)

LEVEL 4: MISSIONS
The final layer is evangelistic missions – periods of concentrated evangelistic activity, with a higher than usual number of events. A mission will have a high profile, both in the community and in the life of the church, and anticipates a large response to the presentation of the gospel message. Our ideas of what a mission is will be coloured by our own experience. For the moment, let us put these ideas to one side, and say that a mission is no longer merely a series of meetings in a large marquee in the centre of town, or a door-to-

door visiting campaign. A mission can take a variety of forms, and use a wide range of evangelistic methods.

THE LONG PROCESS

Conversion is rarely instantaneous. Rather, it is a process which is different for each individual. For most of us, 'conversion' will include a period of searching and enquiring, followed by decision making, and finally growth and nurture. Even Paul had been prepared for the Damascus road episode by his background of strict Judaistic training, and by his contact with Christians as he persecuted them. My own enquiry stage was quite brief because I committed my life to following Christ when I was seven years old. As a result the nurture stage extended over a long period. My 'conversion' lasted throughout my school days, and probably into my time at university. For others, it may be the period of searching that will be longest.

Our evangelism needs to take this process into account. I have found it useful to divide the 'process of evangelism' into five stages:

1. LOCATE
The first step is to find the people we are trying to evangelize. It is pointless evangelizing thin air. I am reminded of the song 'Mission to Seagulls' performed by 70's folk-duo Ishmael and Andy[1]. As the result of a bye-law in force near Bognor Regis, any open-air outreach had to face toward the sea. Unfortunately there were no people on that side of the promenade, only seagulls. Too much of our evangelism fails because we have not located the people. The next chapter will tackle the question of who we should be trying to reach and where to find them.

2. EDUCATE
It is no good expecting people to commit their whole life to something if they do not know what they are letting themselves in for. Did you know that on average a person hears the gospel seven times before making a Christian commitment? I heard this at a training conference several years ago. It was to have a profound influence on my approach to evangelism. It made me realize the vital importance of bringing

people to an *understanding* of Christianity. Education is vital. Many people reject Christianity simply because they do not understand it. They have never been in a position where they have been able to discover the facts for themselves. We should aim to give people enough information so that they can make a reasoned decision whether to accept or reject the gospel.

3. PERSUADE

The 'pivotal point' of conversion is the decision-making. Therefore the critical stage in evangelism is persuasion. It is the Holy Spirit's prerogative to convict people of their sin and to convince them of their need for Christ; the individual's decision is entirely their own. This is not surprising since free will is central to a Christian understanding of God's dealing with his world. Thus, much of this stage of evangelism is out of our hands, although we do have an important role to play. We can provide opportunities for people to be challenged with the gospel during events or as part of evangelistic activities and help them to that point of decision.

4. DISCIPLE

Jesus did not say, 'Go and make converts'. His command is to make disciples. In order to be true to this calling we cannot simply stop at persuasion. We need to help new Christians think and act as Christ instructs. We can do this by helping them to understand what it means to be a Christian and showing them how to live as a follower of Christ. At the very least they must be grounded in the basics of the faith. Sadly, this is probably the stage of evangelism in which we are most ineffective in today's church. In chapter 7 we will look in greater detail at the theory and the practice of discipling.

5. INTEGRATE

A Christian is a child of God and, as such, part of his family. Therefore we need to be totally integrated into that family, the church. This involves learning how to relate to fellow Christians, participating in corporate activities, finding a place in the Body of Christ, and discovering and using gifts and abilities. It is the final stage of evangelism, and it is part of our discipleship. The main difference between this stage and the last is the emphasis: the discipleship could be thought of as our 'vertical' relationship with God, and integration as our 'horizontal' relationship with other Christians. As they are part and parcel of the same process, the division is arbitrary, but I have used it to show that both aspects are vital. One is not complete without the other.

Just as our discipleship will never end as long as we live, neither shall we be totally integrated into God's family until we live with him in eternity. The Bible refers to conversion as 'being saved'. One well known story puts this in the correct perspective: a very keen young Christian sitting in the same railway carriage as a Bishop, leant across and asked him, 'Are you saved?' The Bishop, looking down his nose, replied, 'My dear boy, whatever do you mean? Do you mean have I been saved, am I being saved, or will I be saved?' Of course the Bishop is theologically correct. Salvation is a continuous process; we are still working out our salvation.

All five stages need to feature in our evangelistic endeavours if we are to see people growing into maturity as Christians. Traditionally, evangelistic activity has concentrated on the first three stages: locating people, telling them the gospel, and inviting a response. In this book we will be looking in detail not only at those stages but also at discipleship and integration.

For the rest of this chapter I shall be looking at some of the different activities and types of events that can be used in evangelism. These would fit into level 3 of the diagram on p58. I have (arbitrarily) split them into two categories – evangelistic activities and evangelistic events. An **event** could be a 'one-off' occasion, perhaps involving specialists in an 'up-front' role, although ideally it should be part of a larger programme and involve local Christians. An **activity** would take place over a longer period and those taking part would be, first and foremost, local Christians. The following examples will help to clarify my terminology.

EVANGELISTIC ACTIVITIES

If conversion is a process, then evangelism needs to be viewed in the long term. In chapter 2 we saw that personal witness is the most effective form of evangelism, and this is by its very nature long-term. The types of evangelistic activities in this section should all be an extension of witnessing. Unfortunately, their effectiveness is often severely hampered because they are seen as short-term, or even one-off activities. However, the key to their effectiveness is the building up of relationships which enable the message to be communicated. Most of them involve going to where the people can be found, and are thus much closer to the emphasis of Christ's command to 'Go into all the world. . .'.

DOOR-TO-DOOR VISITING

The very words are guaranteed to strike terror into the hearts of almost any congregation! Door-knocking has the same effect as a trip to the dentist! Yet it is a means of contacting many people who would otherwise never darken the doorstep of their local church. One of the problems with 'door-knocking' is that most Christians fail to realize that there is a wide variety of approaches, some of which are more suited to a particular area or congregation than to others.

The first distinction that needs to be made is between 'cold visiting' and 'contact visiting'. The former involves knocking on every door in the street; the latter, visiting people with whom the church already has contact – maybe they are friends of church members, maybe they have had some fringe involvement in church activities (such as Mothers and Toddlers), perhaps they were married at the church, or possibly they had called on the minister. Whatever the reason, there is a point of contact.

The second distinction concerns the content of the visits. The simplest and least threatening is to introduce the church. For example, on a first visit, members of Ichthus Christian Fellowship in London introduce themselves and their church and then ask if they can help in any way. I have also heard of visits where people are given the opportunity to ask the church to pray for them – if we

really do believe in a God who answers prayer, then this seems very
apt. We can also visit people to invite them along to an event or
special service – Christmas and Easter are obvious opportunities.
Sometimes it is easier to use a tool for evangelism such as a
questionnaire. A word of caution here: we need to be honest and
open. It is not a good witness if we introduce a survey about the
community and at the end try to squeeze the gospel in. It is far better
to say who we are and explain what we are doing, eg 'Hello, I'm from
Hatfield Baptist Fellowship, and we're trying to discover people's
views about religion to help us be more relevant as we talk to people
about our beliefs. Would you help us by answering a few questions
in this survey?'

The other main type of visit is a straightforward presentation of
the gospel message, either on the doorstep or by arranging an
appointment to call back later. Organizations such as 'Mission for
Home Evangelism' and 'Evangelism Explosion' can provide training
and resources for this. (See Appendix 4.)

Any one of these or any combination can form part of a strategy
for door-to-door work. This could also include the use of literature
delivered through the door, or given during the visit. Examples are:
publicity for events, community-type newsletters, a copy of a Gospel,
an evangelistic leaflet (tract), or a letter giving notice of your intention
to visit. As I write this book, I am involved in the planting of a
congregation. We have just delivered leaflets to the area surrounding
our venue to announce the start of the venture. During the rest of
the year we intend to deliver two news-sheets about the congregation
to each house, and to include an invitation to a guest service. We
intend to make personal visits to introduce ourselves during this
period. We shall look into the possibility of delivering Gospels, and
carrying out a survey. The aim is to build up contact so that people
in the community are aware of the fellowship and a relationship can
be built.

We have considered how frightening many Christians find the
thought of door-to-door evangelism, but have not given any attention
to the fear and suspicion that such an approach may cause those who
are being visited – especially if it is cold visiting. We must be
concerned by their fears but this concern should be balanced by the

fact that door-to-door work may be the only way of reaching some people with the gospel. Door-to-door evangelism *may* be inappropriate for some areas, but more often than not the solution is to consider carefully the reactions of householders. While there will be those who do not like what they see as an attempt to interfere in their lives, there will be others who are very grateful for the opportunity to meet and talk to someone. The main lesson is that we must keep the atmosphere light and seek to establish a good rapport, even if it takes months or even years to build on it.

STREET EVANGELISM

This is the second most likely form of evangelism to strike terror into a church meeting! The reason is that we have to make contact from cold, and sometimes our expectation is that we must share the gospel from cold. Some Christians are gifted at this. Most are not. Again, we need to realize that there are different types of street work, each falling into one of two categories – long-term and short-term.

Epping Forest Youth For Christ have developed a model for the former and termed it the street pastor. This involves working in the same area of town on a particular night each week. In this way they build relationships with the youngsters who frequent the streets. As a result they have been able to talk about their faith and invite the kids along to other activities.

Short-term street-work could involve simply stopping people in the street for a conversation with the aim of giving them a leaflet or inviting them along to a subsequent event. Questionnaires can be a useful tool to strike up conversations in this type of situation.

The other main form of street evangelism is proclamation. A variety of media can be used: soap-box preaching; drama; music; conjuring; ventriloquism; the use of visual aids such as sketch-boards whilst preaching. The aim is to attract a crowd, give a brief presentation of the Good News, and offer the opportunity to find out more. Christians who have formed the core of the crowd can then start up conversations with those who stopped to listen. This might be along the lines: 'Hello, I'm with this bunch of people. What did you think about what they were trying to say?' Organizations that can give more help and advice include Open Air Campaigners and Swindon Open Air Project (SOAP) (see Appendix 4). The long-term effectiveness of such evangelism depends on the thorough follow-up of contacts.

COFFEE BARS

This phenomenon of the 1960's is still being used by Christians in various parts of the country. The more enterprising have developed the idea further in order to remain topical. This seems to have worked out in two ways, one retaining the coffee, the other the bar! Coffee shops, either on church or commercial premises, open during the day-time, provide a service to the community and are very useful for making contacts. In my church we have a coffee bar combined with a wholefoods shop. Contacts have been made, relationships built, and some have now come into the church and made a Christian commitment. The other development has been non-alcoholic bars. With the vast range of non-alcoholic beers, wines and cocktails, the possibilities are endless. Many people find a pub atmosphere relaxed and familiar, and so they are more likely to enter into conversation.

The original coffee-bar idea need not die, but it does need dragging into the nineties. The subdued lighting and walls covered in fishing nets need to give way to other decor with themes such as the space-age or hi-tech.

The key to all this is the work of Christians who are prepared to get to know people as they sit at tables, to find out about them and be open to sharing the Good News of Jesus should the opportunity arise. If coffee-bars are used only in the short-term, this work is best supplemented by a musician or drama group that performs for two or three short periods during the evening to act as a focus for conversations.

SCHOOLS WORK

One of the best methods of reaching young people is to gain entry into schools. In this country we are very privileged to have religious assemblies and lessons as a legal requirement. Christians can offer themselves as resources to schools to take part in lessons and assemblies. In so doing they can help young people to understand what it means to be a Christian, and why Christians believe the things they do. They can be thought-provoking. What should not occur during school time is 'persuasion' evangelism in the sense of stage 3 of the process mentioned earlier. Schools are for education, so we should be there to educate (stage 2).

I firmly believe that schools can provide an outstanding opportunity for reaching young people, not to convert them, but to build relationships through regular work in the school, which will act as a foundation for further contact. This is why it is so important that any church considering schools work should be very careful. It is very easy to make an evangelistic foray into a school in such a way that the only lasting result is that Christians will never be allowed to return. Much tact and diplomacy is needed; it is advisable to contact an organization that has a good reputation for its work in schools, such as Scripture Union or British Youth For Christ (see Appendix 4). Be very wary, too, of organizing a visit of schools workers or musicians in isolation from any on-going work, whether that of a teacher in the school, a local worker taking lessons, or an active Christian Union.

If you do intend to work in schools, make sure that you liaise with the other churches in the area. There is nothing worse than duplicating efforts, when you could be working together. Worse still, it confuses the schools.

COLLEGES AND PRISONS

These can also be productive mission fields. It is best to talk with people involved in such work[2] before making any plans. Also be careful not to think solely in terms of outreach events. In colleges the best form of evangelism is through talking to people, not publicizing meetings!

SMALL GROUP EVANGELISTIC BIBLE STUDIES

This is one method advocated by Rebecca Manley Pippert in her classic book on personal evangelism, *Out of the Saltshaker*[3]. It allows people to discover more about Christianity and the person of Jesus Christ by examining the historical documents (ie the Bible) for themselves. Another approach is to ask people if they would like to discover what the Bible has to say about life.

People are confronted by the Word of God, but in such a relaxed setting that they should not feel on edge unless the Holy Spirit is speaking to them. There is a wealth of material available for use in this setting[4].

Neighbourhood Bible studies do not involve going to where others are, but rather inviting neighbours to come into your home. The building of relationships is central to this form of evangelism. A related form of outreach is the **Open House**, where Christians make their home available for people to drop in. They do this as an expression of their open-hearted friendship as they seek to bring people into a loving relationship with Jesus. Such a commitment can involve many sacrifices and needs to be considered thoroughly before starting out.

EVANGELISTIC EVENTS

Evangelism through events alone is often seen as short-term, and can soon become a form of hit-and-run evangelism. If this happens it is a travesty that dishonours a God whose 'evangelistic event' lasted for thirty-three years as he lived amongst us and gave himself for us. An event should ideally be a part of a programme that expresses our commitment to the people we are trying to reach.

It is pointless to have an evangelistic event in isolation. That would mean that there would be no preparation and no follow-up of those who come along. It would be like a pirouette without a ballet, or a musical note without a song. Such an event would risk two major problems: the first being the difficulty of attracting non-Christians along, since there would be little if any contact-building; the second, the lack of follow-up to any response to the evangelistic challenge. An incident from my own experience will best serve to illustrate this point.

I worked on a one-year evangelistic team for British Youth For Christ in the early eighties. We operated in three Bedfordshire villages. Our first outreach activity was to run a coffee bar in each of the villages. At the end of the short run we made a very clear evangelistic challenge. In two of the villages no-one responded; they were not ready to make a commitment since the education stage of evangelism had been squeezed out. In the third village, over half of the young people in the venue made a 'Christian commitment'. Within a few weeks most of them did not want to know: they had backed down. Clearly, they did not have sufficient information on which to base their decision. Those who persevered did so after much effort in follow-up, but even these appear to have drifted away. Others who made a Christian commitment later in the year, and subsequently grew in their faith, were individuals who already had some church background, and with whom we had a large amount of contact leading up to that point of commitment. This underlines the need not only for continuous personal witness, but also for a programme of evangelism in which people are sufficiently informed about the Christian challenge to commitment.

In spite of everything I have said about the need for evangelism to be long-term, there *is* a time when an individual outreach event may be justifiable. This could be when someone would like to mobilize their fellowship into evangelism but is having little success. Organizing an event may help to engender enthusiasm: when people are involved and have seen the outcome, they will want to do more. Every effort has to be made to ensure that preparation, personal invitations to non-Christians, and follow-up arrangements are adequate. In effect the event will prove to be part of a long-term programme if it leads to the church embarking on one.

The following will give some idea of the variety of events that can be used for evangelism:

Music Concerts There are many Christians involved in the music ministry, each with a different style. They range from heavy metal rock bands for young people to middle-of-the-road artistes suitable for a wider audience. In deciding which artistes to use, ask the following questions:

• What kind of audience are you trying to reach? Which age range? How much religious background do they have?

• What style of music would be most suitable in the situation? What quality of presentation?

• What type of venue will be used? Is it acoustically suitable to certain types of music?

- How much equipment can be used in the venue – lights, PA, special effects, etc?
- What kind of evangelistic approach do the artistes have? How will it fit in with your overall plans?

Film Shows There is a large number of Christian films available, although many are of poor quality. A few are of a higher standard, with some suitable for cinema screenings – eg *Jesus, The Prodigal, Cry from the Mountain*, and *John Wycliffe: The Morning Star*. It is also worthwhile considering similar media, such as video, or multi-screen presentations imported from USA. The latter can be very spectacular.

Drama Presentations Christian drama has come on in leaps and bounds over the last decade with companies such as Riding Lights, Footprints and Ambush leading the way. Drama communicates more effectively than music, and appeals to a wider audience than any one particular musical style. Humour, which is prominent in many Christian theatre companies, is a key to effective communication.

Multi-Media Any combination of these art-forms – music, drama, film, etc – can make a very effective presentation. These may be pre-packaged, or you could organize a mix'n'match affair yourself, provided that your planning is both careful and informed.

Whatever events you choose, sooner or later you need to decide whether or not to use a speaker as part of the programme. Sometimes it is out of place: for example, a musician may himself be an effective evangelist; in the case of a film show at a cinema, people would not normally expect to have to sit and listen to a speaker. In other cases an evangelist may be necessary to provide the evangelistic 'punch' for the evening.

FOOD, GLORIOUS, FOOD
Food is a very useful means of attracting people along to events:

Dinner and Cabaret
This can create a very relaxed atmosphere for evangelism to take place. The cabaret can take the form of music, drama, humour, conjuring or even escapology! The choice of venue will be important.

Some churches arrange dinners in local hotels, whilst others cater for themselves on their own premises. The quality of the food, its presentation and the standard of service is vital, so self-catering is only advisable if it can be done well.

After-Dinner Speaker
A variation on the cabaret. Well-known Christians such as TV or sports personalities can be used, or Christians in influential positions in society.

Cheese and Wine/Pizza and Pint Evenings
The choice will depend on the area and what will work best. Again a speaker or an artiste should be central to a gospel presentation.

Coffee Mornings/Supper Parties
These tend to work best in the homes of church members, with a speaker. The low-key approach will link naturally with personal witness.

Barbecues
These work well in the summer months. Again, have some form of entertainment or speaker. Other social activities, such as barn dances, can be a good forum for evangelism. They help to relax people, and to show them that Christians can have fun.

ALL-AGE OUTREACH
The gospel is good news for everyone. It does not matter how old you are or what your situation might be. Our evangelism should reflect the all-embracing aspect of the message.

Families have a special place in God's heart, so some of our activities can aim to reach whole families. A Family Fun Day, involving all kinds of crazy activities: games, especially those with an 'It's a Knockout' flavour, and entertainment, such as ventriloquism and conjuring, could be among the elements for such an event. Sometimes events with a family focus can be linked to children's work such as a holiday club – a week of activities for children organized during school holidays.

Just as there are many people in families, so there are also many without. Events for singles or for the elderly have great potential for evangelism. There is also a need to reach out to specific types of people, especially men. The church has found it notoriously difficult to reach men, so we need to think of events that would appeal to them – a dinner with a speaker can be aimed solely at businessmen, or a pizza and pint evening may be attractive to those who normally frequent the local. People who are keen on sport would be more likely to attend something with a distinctive sporting flavour such as 'A Game of Football with Glenn Hoddle' or similar.

In the past the use of personalities to attract people to an event has worked well. However, not all well-known Christians are evangelists. It may be that some would be far more effective being interviewed in a chat-show format as part of an evangelistic event. It is vital that you discuss your aims and expectations thoroughly with any personality whom you invite to participate in your evangelism, to make sure that they are willing and able to take part in the way you envisage.

STRAIGHT TALKING

Some people will be attracted by straight talking, for example in the form of a talk or a series of talks on Christianity or Christian attitudes, or even a course of lectures or seminars. In the age of the video, we need to recognize that this will not appeal to the majority; nevertheless, a clear presentation of the case for Christianity without any trappings can be the key for certain people to respond to the gospel.

Discussions or debates can also be used. The risk with these is that other points of view will be argued, perhaps persuasively, but if we are convinced of the truth of Christianity then we have nothing to fear. Obviously it is important to find speakers and debaters of a good quality to take part. A competent chairperson is also vital.

A VARIED PROGRAMME

As you can see there is a wide variety of vehicles for evangelism, and this list is by no means exhaustive. Some will work better than others in your particular area. Our choice of methods will depend on a number of factors including our organizational abilities and the resources we have available, bearing in mind the need to produce high quality events that avoid the 'second rate' tag. We will look at these in detail in chapter 8. It will also depend on the people we are trying to reach with the Good News of Jesus Christ. That is the subject of our next chapter.

In this chapter we have begun to think about what is involved in evangelism, and some of the specific activities we can use in our outreach. We should try to be innovators too – why should we always copy the world? Why not be trend-setters? In its early days, British Youth For Christ had a motto: 'Geared to the times, anchored to the Rock'. This is equally valid for today's Church: we must reach out to the people who need Christ in their lives *by all means*.

| NOTES |

1. From the album *The Charge of the Light Brigade* recorded by Ishmael on the Dovetail label (Catalogue no. Dove 31).

2. For example: Prison Fellowship; David Stillman Association. See Appendix 4 for addresses.

3. *Out of the Saltshaker*, Rebecca Manley Pippert (IVP, 1980)

4. *Jesus: One of Us*, A Lum & B Kristensen (IVP, 1981)
The Man from Outside, G Bridger (IVP, 1978)
Suitable material is also produced by UCCF and Navpress among others. See Appendix 4 for addresses.

| SUMMARY |

• There are four building blocks to church-based evangelism:

  □ on-going personal witness,
  □ evangelistic emphasis in church activities,
  □ programme of evangelistic events,
  □ evangelistic missions.

These should all be based on a foundation of prayer.
• Evangelism is a five-stage process:

  □ *locate* your target audience,
  □ *educate* them about the gospel,
  □ *persuade* them to commit their lives to Christ,

□ *disciple* them into the faith,
□ *integrate* them into the church.

● A wide variety of events and activities can be used for evangelism:
□ Activities include: door-to-door evangelism; street evangelism; coffee-bars; schools work; colleges and prisons; evangelistic Bible studies, open home.
□ Events must be part of long-term programme. They include concerts; films; drama presentations; meals; lectures; seminars; debates; discussion groups.
Events can be aimed at particular age ranges and circumstances.

| ACTION SHEET 3 |

EXERCISE 1

15 MINUTES – In groups of four or five, relate experiences of different methods of evangelism. Discuss their effectiveness in those particular situations. Discuss the reasons for their success or failure. How appropriate would they be for your area?

EXERCISE 2

20 MINUTES – In groups of three or four, use the list of events and activities in chapter 3 as a basis for discussing which methods of evangelism could be used by your church. Use a table like that overleaf. Against each method, list any positive or negative factors that should be taken into account when deciding whether or not to use them.

10 MINUTES – Share ideas with whole group. Leaders should note good ideas.

PREPARATIONS

Methods of evangelism	Negative factors	Positive factors
EXAMPLE: Youth coffee bar	No suitable venue belonging to church. Difficult to find youth leaders in church, etc.	Church member willing to allow use of room above shop. Enthusiastic youth group, etc.

CHAPTER FOUR

WHERE HAVE ALL THE PEOPLE GONE?

WHO ARE WE TRYING TO REACH?

We need to be appropriate in our choice of methods of reaching out to people with the good news of Jesus. Our choice of methods for outreach will depend on the people and other resources we have available, and most importantly, on the people we are trying to reach. It is to this second factor that we shall now turn our attention.

Much of our evangelism fails because we try to cast the net too wide. Often our evangelistic efforts are aimed at the very broad target of 'the people out there', 'the unsaved', or 'those who live in darkness'. Our aim is too vague. We need to be specific, and realize that different evangelistic methods are suited to different people. If we use a heavy metal rock concert as an outreach, we will probably attract only those who like that particular style of music. This is fine if that is our main target area, but if our target includes families and elderly folk we will be extremely unlikely to interest them, let alone attract any to the event.

When the disciples were instructed by Jesus to be his witnesses, he gave them a strategy. They were to work 'in Jerusalem, in all Judea and Samaria, and to the ends of the earth' (Acts 1:8). Their mission would follow the pattern of ripples created by a stone falling into water, moving from the centre outwards. In much the same way, our work must begin at home and spread outwards. There are people who need to hear the gospel in our churches, among our natural contacts, and beyond.

EVANGELISM IN THE CHURCH

Even in the most evangelistic of churches there will be people who involve themselves in church activities but have never committed their lives to following Christ. They might do all the right things in all the right places and so give the impression of being a Christian, and yet they have not made a personal decision to commit their lives to God. Some will have been holding out against God's claim on their lives for years, and others will have recently come into the orbit of the church without a personal faith. These people need evangelizing just as much as any others.

There are two approaches to working among them. The first is to 'target' them for evangelism; the second is to involve them in the evangelism of the church, so that as a by-product they will respond to the gospel. Both methods have their difficulties.

By specifically aiming evangelism at such people, we run the risk of their feeling 'got at'. Yet sometimes it is right to help people face up to the command of Jesus Christ to 'follow me'. Sometimes we need to sit down with them and spell out the gospel message in simple terms, making sure they understand. Perhaps they have never really understood before. This is not the right approach with everyone, though, and some would feel bitter and resentful in that position. Another approach which is less pressurizing is to organize group activities for people in the same boat, and as time progresses encourage group members to express their feelings and reservations. This could operate as an 'Agnostics Anonymous' group, although the use of such a name may not be advisable. Activities could vary from purely social events to discussions and Bible studies.

The second approach, that of uncommitted people helping practically at evangelistic events and activities, can result in difficult situations such as a conversation that might arise with an outsider who expresses an interest in the gospel. However, Christianity is about acceptance, and we must express that in the way we involve people in the life of the church. The leaders of any activity will not only need to be aware of the problem, but will also need to be very sensitive towards non-Christians who are helping, and the situations in which they become involved.

In the preparation for the 'Mission England' and 'Mission to London' activities in the early 1980's, courses were run to train Christians to talk to those who responded to the gospel appeal at the main meetings, and to help with follow-up. Organizers were delighted to discover that people were actually becoming Christians at these training events – something that had not been envisaged. This shows that the more people hear the gospel, the more likely they are to respond. Their involvement in evangelistic events will put them in a position to hear presentations of the gospel message.

NATURAL CONTACTS

Natural contacts fall into two categories: those in contact with individuals and those with the church. These are the people who are within reach, since they have already established relationships with members of the church.

CONTACTS WITH INDIVIDUALS

Contacts with individuals include personal friends, colleagues, acquaintances and relatives of church members. If witnessing is part of the life of the church, they will probably have had some contact with the gospel. Any evangelistic effort from the church needs to capitalize on this, and to act as a resource for that witness. At a recent house group meeting, for example, we listed all the people with whom we had contact locally, and from that list decided on the best methods for reaching them. This has a twofold effect: it encourages church members to ask their contacts along to something specifically designed for them, and encourages those who mistakenly thought there was no-one left for them to witness to.

CONTACTS WITH THE CHURCH

Church contacts provide another large mission field. These may include parents of children who attend church activities, those who have been married at the church, relatives of those who have been buried, parents of children who have been dedicated, christened or confirmed, those who have attended activities such as Mothers and Toddlers, those who used to attend youth groups, those who have sought counselling with the minister – the list is almost endless. All of them will have some sympathy with the aims of the church, to a greater or lesser extent. With few exceptions, this will be an advantage, since there will be some common ground.

Relationships can be built through further visits, or by personal invitation to specific events. A reunion for a youth group will guarantee an interesting and varied collection of people who may have drifted away from the church. The offer of a marriage enrichment evening to couples whose wedding took place at the church may also result in renewed contact. It can be difficult to get people along to events, visiting them is most likely to produce results. Visiting should not be left to the minister; there is plenty of scope for involving other church members. Make the choice of visitors carefully. They will have a great opportunity to build a friendship, and to be able to witness through that relationship. Visits need not be made with the initial aim of getting people involved in the church, but rather to find out how they are, and if there is any way in which the church can help them.

I consistently find that with any group of Christians, the majority have had connections with the church in their childhood or youth. This is an encouragement to make the most of following up those who have had church connections in the past. This natural point of contact can give a head-start in building relationships.

BEYOND THE DOUGHNUT

It may be easier to reach people who are within the church's circle of 'natural' contacts than those beyond, but if the church concentrated solely on those people, it would fail to make much of an impact on society. Only a fraction of the population in any particular area would be reached. When we look at the numbers who have contact with the church under normal circumstances, it is a very small proportion. Swindon, for example, has 30 evangelical churches and a 200-year history of evangelicalism. Those churches are in regular contact with only 750 young people out of a total of almost 26,000[1]. This led author and evangelist John Allan to write an article called 'Beyond the doughnut' in which he suggests that the church is surrounded by a soft 'doughnut' of contacts. These people often have a religious background, but beyond them is the 'real non-Christian world'.

'It is possible,' he writes, 'to be seeing packed rallies, successful clubs, over-subscribed camps and houseparties – and yet be failing to reach the real world. It is possible for us to spend enormous amounts of time, energy and dollars – and yet end up talking only to a tiny circle of people remarkably like ourselves. How do we break through the doughnut? How do we make sure we reach the truly unreached?'[2]

First, we need to discover as much as we can about the area in which we are to be working in order to obtain an accurate picture. Even though we may have lived in an area for years, our knowledge will be incomplete and probably one-sided.

SURVEYING THE LAND

The three main sources of information about any locality will be: official statistics and reports; questionnaire surveys among the people; talking with those 'in the know', such as police officers, council officials, etc.

STATISTICS, REPORTS AND MAPS

Statistics and reports should be available in the reference section of the local library, or alternatively at the local council offices. Local history societies are also a useful source. These will provide you with information such as total population, types of housing, lists of amenities, crime statistics, etc. The latest census information, although dealing with large areas, can also be very revealing.

Maps can sometimes shed light on divisions in the area such as boundary lines. In Welwyn Garden City, for example, the railway has historically been such a dividing line. On the one side is the town centre and a predominantly middle class residential area; on the other side are the industrial areas, large stretches of council housing, and a high proportion of single-parent families and people with broken marriages. The former is a Conservative/Democrat held area, the latter, Labour held. Any evangelism in the town has to take this into account. Within these main areas there are smaller, well-defined communities such as Panshanger which is quite separate from the town centre, and consists mainly of newly married couples and young families.

QUESTIONNAIRES

Questionnaires should aim to gather information about the type of people, their attitudes and their activities. Questions about the numbers in the household, how long they have been living there, the type of work members of the family are involved in, and observations on the age of the person questioned will provide a good start in discovering more about residents. It may be that in a particular area, most people are on shift work. This has implications for the time to hold events and the size of attendance it is reasonable to expect. Questions about hobbies and use of leisure time are also useful. If this is used in conjunction with information about local leisure facilities, it is fairly easy to build up a picture of where people can be found when not at work.

It is also helpful to ask for people's comments on the needs of the area. This gives an indication of what can be usefully done by the church to express God's love in a caring and practical way – the broader aspect of mission. If for example there are found to be large numbers of addicts in the area, some form of counselling service may be of benefit to the community and a means of making contact with those who are normally outside the scope of a church. If, on the other hand, it is discovered that there are a large number of young families on an estate, a Mother and Toddler group would meet a need. Beware of the danger of becoming involved in special needs at the expense of reaching the wider majority of people, however. You will need to weigh this up against all the other factors involved.

KEY PEOPLE

Some people will, by virtue of their particular job or their personality, have inside knowledge of the community. The police, for example, will know of problems that affect particular areas. One local bobby near to our church was aware of the need for a youth club as a result of increased vandalism, complaints from people about teenagers, and talking with the young people as he met them on his beat. As a result, the church has set up a youth club as its main form of youth outreach. Council officials will also have some local knowledge, as will hairdressers and pub landlords who spend much of their time in conversation with their clientele.

Accurate information about the locality will help shape our evangelism, and increase its effectiveness. As a result of gathering such information you will be in a position to discard certain styles of evangelism as being irrelevant in your case. You will have a much better idea of where to find the people that you want to reach.

WHERE THEY'RE AT!

Each locality is different from the next, but there are national trends that we need to take into account as we plan our evangelism.

In our outreach to adults we need to discover the best environment to meet people and build contacts. Is the British public to be found in the local pub? The answer is yes, but not all at the same time. Recent surveys[3] show that only 75% of households spend money on alcohol. 30% of this is for consumption at home. Even when all the pubs are crowded, there are far more adults at home than out drinking. There needs to be outreach to pubs and clubs, but we need to be aware of the vast numbers who remain at home.

A major trend over the last 25 years has been the increase in leisure time. People are working fewer hours and have longer holidays than ever before. This could provide great opportunities for reaching people, so we need to discover how they use their leisure time. National surveys show that men use 25 hours each week to watch television in addition to the time watching videos. Women spend 30 hours in front of the TV. We need to investigate the effect that this will have on door-to-door work – will it be seen as an invasion of privacy, especially in the middle of an episode of *Eastenders* or *Neighbours*? Could we use this phenomenon to our advantage by using videos as a major part of our evangelism? Between 1984 and 1986 the number of households with a video recorder increased from 20% of the population to 33%.[4]

The way we use literature in evangelism should reflect the reading habits of people. The most popular daily newspaper is The Sun, which is not noted for its literary style! Our leaflets should reflect this in areas where the tabloid press is predominant.

In mid–1987, 3.2 million people were registered as unemployed. In some areas of the country the unemployment rate is very high. This unfortunate circumstance could be used as the basis for evangelism. Day-time activities for the unemployed, or help with searching for jobs, will not only provide a much needed service, but will also bring people into contact with the church.

GO . . .

We may have problems locating the people we are trying to reach but one thing is certain: the vast majority of them are not in churches! Jesus commanded his followers to 'go'. He did not instruct us to invite people along to meetings, or to even expect people to come in. His command is to look outward, rather than inward. Jesus himself gives a perfect example.

God himself became a man in order to live among mankind. He did not stay in the heavenly realms; instead he left the glory of heaven to be born as an ordinary mortal. It does not end with the incarnation. Jesus spent much of his time going to live among the dregs of society, those who were despised by the religious authorities and decent citizens: the tax-collectors, prostitutes and beggars. Jesus was known as the 'friend of sinners'; and he came not to be served, but to serve. He was not afraid of getting his hands dirty. He exemplified what God expects of us.

In our evangelism, once we have discovered where people are, we must not resort to mere forays into their world. We need to get alongside people, to share their worries and hurts, to help them when it counts, and to identify with them. This is not a cheap evangelism: it can cost much in terms of time, money and reputation. This is the side of evangelism that lacks any real glamour, and yet it is vital if we are to reach the unreached.

IN A CLASS OF THEIR OWN

The church in Britain appears to be predominantly middle-class. It is strongest in middle-class areas of the country. The British equivalent of the Bible Belt runs through the commuter lands of Surrey. The emphasis on personal faith and fulfilment appeals to the exam-passing, upwardly mobile, as opposed to the working class where group solidarity matters far more than any individual achievement. The proliferation of Christian books and the emphasis on the written word runs against vast numbers of people in whose homes a book would be out of place.

In his masterly though highly underrated book, *Urban Harvest*[5], Roy Joslin deals extensively with this problem. He quotes Dr Martin Lloyd Jones from a paper delivered in 1975: 'The impression has gained currency that to be a Christian, and more especially an evangelical, means that we are traditionalists, and advocates of the status quo. I believe that this largely accounts for our failure in this country to make contact with the so-called working classes. Christianity has become a middle class movement. . . .'[6]

The image of a church restricted to the middle classes must be changed. We need to reach out into a community that can be suspicious of outsiders, and where loyalty to one's own is uppermost. In order to do this the British church must face up to three challenges.

A CHALLENGE TO OUR COMMUNICATION

A major barrier to evangelism is the excessive emphasis on words, and the accompanying intellectualism. For a large section of the community, the most effective communication is visual. We live in a video age, in which the image is the message. Pop records no longer sell purely because of the tune and the lyrics, but because of the video that promotes the song.

Many people have difficulty in grasping abstract concepts. They need to have ideas spelt out in concrete terms that can be understood. The concepts of salvation and atonement need to be illustrated by stories and visual aids. Overhead projector illustrations take the place of stained glass windows that were designed to express spiritual truths and Bible stories to a different generation of people.

There are a large number of people who do not want to be convinced by clever argument and intellectual reasoning; it is experience that will be the decisive factor for them.

The challenge to the church is whether we will continue to rely on lecture-style preaching, or whether we will master the art of illustration and the use of visual aids; whether we continue to appeal solely to the intellect, or whether we reach out to God to act in the lives of ordinary people, even to the extent of expecting miracles which will point people towards God.

A CHALLENGE TO OUR CREDIBILITY

The media image of Christianity has been poor throughout this century. Ministers are portrayed as weak, insipid, doddery old men with buck teeth, forever offering cucumber sandwiches. Churches are shown as being populated by a few very serious men wearing black suits and carrying big black Bibles under their arms, amongst a plethora of old women and young children. Such images lack 'street-credibility'.

The 'man in the street' needs to see that a Christian can be a 'real man'. Every vestige of the wimp image needs to be discarded. Christians need to show that they are living in the real world, and that their heads are not stuck in the clouds. Moreover the church must show to the world that Christianity works. In the early church, Tertullian records how it was the strong love amongst Christians that made an impact even on its critics. Christian love flows out of Jesus' love. It was tough love. He did not let anyone down. You could rely on him in every situation. Our love for others needs to be like that.

A CHALLENGE TO OUR STRUCTURES

Many church services seem irrelevant to the outsider. The traditions are rooted in past centuries, most of the hymns are at least a hundred years old. They could be forgiven for thinking they had entered a time-warp! It would be very interesting to ask someone who has little idea of what happens in church to give an honest critique. I suspect we would find it revealing and refreshing, if not a little threatening.

We need to look critically at our ways of communicating. The attention span of most people is less than ten minutes, and yet the minimum sermon length in most churches is twenty minutes. We need to examine the structure of our meetings as well. Why are we meeting together? One certain way of throwing a meeting into confusion is to ask that question. The next thing to ask is whether the meeting is fulfilling that purpose. Asking such questions may seem provocative but it may result in a progressive and constructive attitude towards existing meetings, and a healthy desire to change.

Reaching out beyond the doughnut is a daunting task, but if we are to have any hope of changing the spiritual climate in Britain, we need to make inroads into non-Christian territory. That will mean targetting our evangelism, and it may well mean changes in the way we do things.

| NOTES |

1. *Beyond the Doughnut*, John Allan, YFCI World Perspective vol 4 No 3

2. Ibid

3. *Family Expenditure Survey 1986*, Department of the Environment, published by Government Statistical Service

4. *Social Trends 18*, Central Statistical Office. Subsequent figures are also from this source.

5. *Urban Harvest*, Roy Joslin (Evangelical Press, 1982)

6. *The Christian and the State in Revolutionary Times*, Dr M Lloyd Jones (Westminster Conference, 1975) p103

| SUMMARY |

● Our methods of evangelism must be appropriate to those we are trying to reach, and this means we must define the groups we wish to target.

They will include:
- people in the church,
- those with whom the church has natural contacts,
- those beyond the church's natural contacts.

● We need to gather information about our locality through:
- statistics, reports and maps,
- surveys,
- key people in the area.

● We need to be aware of regional and national trends in behaviour.
● We need to go to people where they are.
● The church has generally failed to make a significant impact on the working classes. This has a challenge for:
- our communication,
- our credibility,
- our structures.

| ACTION SHEET 4 |

SESSION A

EXERCISE 1
15 MINUTES – In groups of four or five, 'brainstorm' information about the locality. (See the note in Exercise 5 of Action Sheet 1 for instructions on brainstorming.) One person in the group should write down everything that is said during the brainstorming.

15 MINUTES – Sift through this information, putting it into some kind of order. Apply the following questions to each piece of information:
- Is the information accurate? Is it an impression? Is it hearsay?
- To what proportion of the local population does this apply?
- What are the implications for evangelism?

15 MINUTES – Collate and compare information from each group.

EXERCISE 2: ACTION EXTRA
15 MINUTES – ORGANIZE:
- two groups to do a statistical survey. One group will be finding out about the church congregation, the other about the town or the immediate area. Find out how many men and women fall into the following age brackets: 0–10; 11–20; 21–30; 31–40; 41–50; 51–60; 61+. (You may find that these age brackets are inconvenient if,

for example, local statistics are available in other ranges.) Work out the ethnic breakdown of your church and the community in a similar fashion, but make sure that this is done very sensitively.

Transfer the information into diagrammatic form using bar-charts or pie-charts. You may need someone with an understanding of statistics to do this and also to ensure that you use the available information correctly.

Compare the information for the church with that of the community.
□ someone to co-ordinate a list of addresses of church members (divided into area or house groups as appropriate).
Both sets of information will be needed for the next session.

SESSION B

EXERCISE 3
15 MINUTES – As a group, study a street map of the area. Discuss ideas concerning the various features (main roads, rivers, railways, estate boundaries, etc) that act as barriers in the community. Mark on the map those over which there is general agreement.

Plot the position of churches on the map. Discuss the centres of community activities (schools, sports centres, shopping parades, leisure facilities, etc), and mark them on the map. Finally, using the information collated since the last session, plot the location of church members' homes, and homes used for house groups. Make sure that each category is marked with a different coloured symbol.

10 MINUTES – In small groups, discuss any salient features of your coded map. For example:
□ Where are church members clustered together?
□ Where is there only a sprinkling?
□ Are there any particular areas of town that you could target for evangelism where there is no church in the vicinity?
□ Are you working in the area surrounding your own church?
□ How could you work in the centres of activity in the community?

EXERCISE 4
20 MINUTES – Present the information about age/sex/ethnic breakdown of the congregation and the district. In groups of four or five, note where there are major differences in the proportions in each category. Discuss whether you

87

should work from strength in your evangelism (ie, if you have strength in a certain age range in the church, to concentrate evangelistic efforts among their peers), or whether to make a priority of evangelizing amongst those ranges who are missing in church. List the positive and negative factors that will affect your planning.

EXERCISE 5

15 MINUTES – As a whole group, spend five minutes or so brainstorming about the different lifestyles of the people in your area, eg DIY fanatics who spend all their time making alterations to their houses; computer buffs who have in effect created a leisure centre in their own home; the farming community; inner city youth; etc.

Divide into groups of four or five to brainstorm methods of evangelism that will reach people with the lifestyles mentioned. Encourage innovation by writing down even the most unusual ideas. Some will be worthwhile pursuing in order to reach those who may currently be beyond the church's influence.

YOU IN YOUR SMALL CORNER

INVOLVING THE WHOLE CHURCH IN EVANGELISM

The church is called to evangelism, and there are some Christians who are specifically gifted by God to be evangelists. However, every member can be directly involved in the church's evangelistic activities. It seems strange that even in churches where evangelistic efforts are few and far between, any activity that does reach out into the community is so often kept under wraps. When so few members are aware of what is happening, it will probably lack essential prayer support and interest.

A major priority in our evangelism must be to involve the whole of the church. We need to ensure that everyone is kept informed, and that as many people as possible are given the opportunity to be involved. This must be done in an orderly manner. It would be hopeless if everyone involved themselves in any evangelistic activities that came their way, without some measure of co-ordination and direction. This is one area in which witnessing and evangelism differ. There can never be enough personal witnessing, but in order for evangelism to be most effective it needs a strategy, some kind of agreed agenda whereby the church membership knows what it is doing. The alternative is chaos.

ALL OVER THE PLACE!

Imagine the confusion: no-one really knows exactly what is happening and what is not happening. Individuals find themselves either committed to too many activities, which results in a clash of loyalties, or not involved in anything. Different evangelistic activities booked for the same day are followed by a long period of inactivity. Any activity that does take place will barely scratch the surface. The church is all over the place in the worst sense!

This is a very poor witness to the world. Not only are we called as individuals to be witnesses, but the church as a whole is a witness. When people look at the church they are in effect looking at the Body of Christ. If they see a church that is pulling in many different directions at the same time, with no co-ordination or cohesion, what impression will they have of Jesus?

Jesus' prayer before his crucifixion was that his followers would be one, and that they would act in unity: 'May they be brought to complete unity to let the world know that you sent me and have loved them even as you have loved me' (John 17:23). Our thoughtlessness, particularly in our lack of a strategy, prevents Jesus' desire being fulfilled.

I know that my body can only do one job at a time well. As soon as I try to do more than one thing problems arise – I lose my concentration or my balance and the job is botched. Of course, this does not mean that every part of my body is directly involved in that job, but there does need to be co-ordination. It is not surprising, then, that when Paul describes the church as the Body of Christ he is most insistent that every member has a role to play. The members of the Body depend on each other; each is as important as the next. Any activity, however praiseworthy it may seem, that disrupts the unity of the Body and the interdependence of its members, thwarts the purpose of the church.

God always has good reasons for his instructions. The reasons for unity are very clear in the context of evangelism. If members of a church are pulling in different directions, the evangelism will lose much of its real impact and run the risk of becoming totally ineffective. In most cases, a church's resources are stretched even in its normal activities. When evangelism is added, those resources can become over-stretched, particularly when co-ordination is lacking. Evangelism needs to be a concentrated effort. It needs concentrated prayer to protect it against all that Satan might do to undermine its effectiveness.

There are measures that can be taken to reduce the likelihood of our evangelistic effort becoming a fiasco.

WHAT'S COOKING?

In all our talk about organizing evangelistic activities we must never forget that evangelism is taking place in our normal church programme. Look back at the diagram on p58 – many of our church activities have potential for an evangelistic emphasis, which I called level 2 of evangelism. The danger is that often we do not realize that it is happening, or even if we do, we fail to capitalize on its potential by giving it due attention.

Many churches run mother and toddler groups which attract mums who do not attend the church. This is potentially an evangelistic event. The Christians who attend need to realize this – they can then work at building friendships with the mums who come along, and through that friendship speak to them about Jesus, and invite them along to other activities. Others in the church need to realize the potential – they can pray for the activity, for the Christians as they witness, and for the non-Christians who attend. They can also encourage the leaders of the group, by expressing their interest in the group's progress.

Some churches have 'gospel' services each week, where the main thrust is evangelistic. In fact, if no newcomers are in the service, this may have less potential than the mother and toddler group. What is the point of preaching to the converted? However, if the emphasis was changed to worship or teaching, a quarterly or monthly 'Guest Service' to which Christians are encouraged to bring their friends would make more impact. This works best when personal witness is happening day by day, and when those responsible for the service don't try too hard! There is nothing more off-putting to a casual visitor in a church service than to have the feeling that they are being 'got at' by everyone else there. It is the Holy Spirit who convicts people of their sin, and convinces them of their need for Christ. Our role in our services is to proclaim and explain the gospel, and to show others what it is like to be a Christian – for example, that we can enjoy praising God. An evangelistic service is one in which everything is geared to those who are not familiar with our traditions, our jargon and the good news of Jesus Christ. We need to move far beyond the notion that only 'hell-fire and brimstone' sermons are truly evangelistic.

The two criteria that can be used in determining whether an activity is evangelistic are:
● Do non-Christians take part? Would it be practical/easy for non-Christians to participate?
● Are there opportunities to share the gospel of Jesus Christ, either informally or as part of the programme?

Once this has been established, we must then determine the effectiveness of the evangelism. If the effectiveness is already high, or can be improved to a reasonable level, we are then in a position to include these activities in our programme of evangelism, and to support them prayerfully and practically. This will help to avoid duplicating and overstretching resources.

MAKING THE DECISIONS

Evangelism needs to be co-ordinated, but who should that co-ordinator be? Should it be just one person, or a group of people, or yet another committee? How much should the church leaders be involved? All of these questions are valid for individual events and long-term programmes.

QUALITIES OF AN EVANGELISM CO-ORDINATOR

It is unwise to appoint someone who is gifted as an evangelist as the co-ordinator of your programme. The reason for this is simple: most evangelists are lousy administrators! The gifts of an evangelist are rarely those needed for organizing evangelism: they can do it, but cannot necessarily organize it! The qualities of a co-ordinator include:
● The ability to see evangelism in its widest sense, and to think strategically.

• The ability to plan activities and to organize people. Delegation is a useful skill, as is administration.
• A heart for evangelism. Although he or she does not have to be an evangelist, there must be the desire to see men and women come into the kingdom of God.
• Ability that commands the respect and trust of the church leadership. It is useless appointing someone who then has to fight every step of the way to gain the approval of the church leaders over every little decision.
• The ability to motivate people to evangelism is useful, though not essential if there is someone else who can fulfil that role.

INDIVIDUAL OR GROUP?
'Too many cooks spoil the broth', but on the other hand, 'two heads are better than one'. A small team of carefully selected people with one recognized leader is probably best. It is unwise to have a large group of people since that can dilute energy and enthusiasm. There is also a tendency to talk round in circles when more than three or four people are involved. The small group is preferable since it allows ideas to be bounced around, and yet is small enough to be decisive. In general, the larger the group, the greater the internal wrangling.

Ideally, an evangelism co-ordination group should include a visionary who can dream big dreams, and can see potential where others might not. It should also include someone who is down-to-earth and very practical so that potential obstacles and problem areas can be spotted in advance.

LEADERS' INVOLVEMENT
If a member of the church leadership is involved, it shows the importance attached to evangelism, and this will be reflected in the response from the church as a whole. It will also cut out one stage in the decision-making process. On the other hand, the leader (whether vicar, minister or elder, full or part-time) will probably be very busy with other aspects of running the church, and this may only add to his or her burden. He or she may not have the necessary qualities to be effective in such a role. Leaders are just as human

as anyone else, with strengths and weaknesses. It would be counter-productive to include the church leader in the group if this is the case.

A church may arrive at the point where it would be worthwhile appointing someone as evangelism co-ordinator in a full-time capacity. This is a role which any church committed to evangelism should consider seriously, however far in the future such an appointment might lie.

AVOIDING THE PITFALLS

The co-ordinator, or co-ordinating group, should be in a position to steer clear of the problems outlined earlier in the chapter. Without such authority their effectiveness will be considerably limited.

The starting point is to survey the current evangelistic activity in the church and gain an accurate idea of its current effectiveness and its potential for achieving its goals. The number of people involved and the amount of resources used should also be noted. Once this has been done, two key questions should be asked:

1. Are there any activities that are working at cross-purposes? For example, there may be two women's organizations in the church, both with potential to reach a large number of women, and yet there is little communication between the two. Each is run by a different set of women; each buys its own supply of tea and coffee; each has its own urn that is idle when the other organization meets. They meet at the same time but on different days with the room less than half full. Expressed in this way it is fairly obvious that something needs to be done.

2. Are any individuals overtaxed by their involvement in activities? Most churches suffer from this problem: a few do everything, and many do nothing. Eventually the few will become exhausted, perhaps disillusioned, and their activities will suffer accordingly. A co-ordinator needs to recognize who the key people are. They will be people who are particularly talented in certain areas, especially areas where there is a dearth of people who can do the job satisfactorily. When the key people have been found, the co-ordinator needs to work out where they could best be utilized, without overloading them. They should then concentrate on those areas, leaving the co-ordinator to find others to cover the remaining jobs. For example, someone may be an excellent communicator, but most of her time is spent co-ordinating activities. In this case it would be more effective to hand over the co-ordination to someone else, while she concentrates on speaking at events and taking part in door-to-door evangelism.

These two steps will go some way to tackling the problem of the church pulling in too many directions at the same time. The other vital steps are to formulate a strategy and plan the programme of outreach. These steps will be discussed in detail in chapter 6.

BOTH HANDS KNOW!

One of the weakest areas in church life is that of communication.[1] We often fail to communicate effectively with the outside world, which is the reason for writing this book, but we are sometimes even worse when it comes to communicating within the church. It is not unusual for the right hand not to know what the left is doing.

Internal communication is vital for two reasons. Firstly, we need to keep people informed, so that they are aware of church activities. This will enable them to be more specific in their intercessions – a mark of effective prayer. Secondly, we can encourage others to involve themselves in activities. It is very sad to see the way some activities struggle on year after year. The leaders become increasingly bitter that no-one offers any help, and yet they have never made the effort to communicate their need for assistance. It is equally sad when a plea for help is made, but is not communicated in the most effective way, so again there is no response.

There are two particular problems that hinder communication: blockages and blindness.

A **blockage** occurs when, for one reason or another, a piece of information fails to reach its destination. It may end up at the bottom of a pile of 'important' correspondence or worse still in the rubbish bin. At some point there is a breakdown in communication, so the message does not get through. The fault may lie with an individual or with a system. In both cases it needs to be pinpointed and resolved. If an individual is blocking communication, that person may need to be by-passed and an alternative, more reliable route found. This is a short-term solution. Some questions will need to be asked about that person's need to do this, and the situation sensitively resolved, if at all possible by church leaders. If it is a system which is proving ineffective, that system may need to be changed. In my communication with local churches when I worked for Youth for Christ, I aimed to find reliable people who would literally put our news bulletins into the hands of those people who were likely to be interested, rather than leaving them in a neat but dusty pile at the back of the church vestibule.

Blindness hinders communication, not in its literal sense but with equally devastating results! I am constantly amazed at how little people take in when reading notice-sheets or looking at notice-boards (if they get as far as actually looking). This shows how important it is to make notices stand out. In the end, we cannot rely totally on written information; there needs to be a personal contact.

Let's now look at the various ways information can be passed on in a church situation.

SPREAD THE NEWS

NOTICE-BOARDS

Church notice-boards are often dull, untidy, or both. This is a sweeping generalization, but it is based on observation. Notice-boards suffer from a proliferation of printed notices, often in such small type that they can only be deciphered from a distance of six inches. How can this be remedied?

It is best to appoint someone to take responsibility for all the notice-boards in the church. They should be organized and ruthless, with an eye for good presentation. The notice-board should be inspected regularly, at least once a week, to remove notices that are out-of-date. Next, the number of posters and leaflets that are destined for the notice-board needs to be cut down. A large proportion should be rejected: some will be unsuitable, and others will be relevant for a mere handful of people, and should be directed to them rather than displayed. Leaflets that are supposed to be read carefully would be better placed in leaflet holders, so that they can be taken away from the board.

A good notice or poster will be simple and informative, with the important information in print large enough to be read from a few feet away. A good display makes good use of the space available, and leaves sufficient space to make it attractive. It is a good idea to have several notice-boards, each for a different purpose. In our church, for example, one board is reserved for a display for the various mission activities that are supported (the display changes each month), one for church notices, and one for community information. There is still room for improvement, but this is at least a start. A regular change of a main display ensures that people look at the notice-board more regularly than if the notices are several years old!

CHURCH MAGAZINES

In the past, church newsletters have often had a reputation for shoddy production. This is becoming less so, particularly since the cost of owning or renting a photocopier has come within the reach of an average-sized church. Even if one church cannot obtain a copier, it is feasible to co-operate with nearby churches or Christian organizations[2]. Articles in the newsletter are very useful for reaching most people in the church with reasonable amounts of information. However, there are ways of ensuring that a greater percentage of people will actually read those articles.

Firstly, an article needs to be economical in its content. The shorter it is, the more likely it is to be read. If it is long, (150 words or more) it will need headings or graphics to break it up into manageable chunks, and columns rather than full-width text. Avoid very small type and make sure the headline is bold. If your newsletter is normally reduced from A4 originals to A5, it is better to use an A5 original so that no reduction is necessary. I would never suggest reducing by more than one fifth. If you are leading up to an event you should consider a number of smaller contributions over several editions, maybe written by different people, certainly presented in different styles, so that there is variety.

NEWS-SHEETS

In many churches, weekly news-sheets are now used as the main form of notices. These should be used, but bear in mind that one notice among many others will lose its impact, unless it is made to stand out. Methods for achieving this include: the use of graphics; the use of borders; the use of witty or eye-catching text.

LETTERS

Occasionally, the use of a letter to church members, addressed individually, will convey the importance of its contents. These should be used sparingly, since 'familiarity breeds contempt'. Again, be brief, but be informative.

IN PERSON

All of the above are useful ways of communicating information and asking for help, but they can easily be overlooked by the very people that you want to take notice. I often hear the plaintive cry of an organizer, 'It's been on the notice-board and in the news-sheet, so they should have known about it!' They probably should, but the most effective way of communicating with people is to do it in person.

In public

This can be done in church services, housegroups, or other meetings in the church. It is best done by someone other than the usual notice-giver. They need to be brief and to the point, and yet make an impact. Think carefully what needs to be said and how to present it. If you are not used to giving notices it is best to write it out in full, or at least in note-form, and practise beforehand. Long-winded, waffly notices will discourage people from listening and taking them in. Most notices should be shorter than two minutes (occasionally up to five minutes can be given over to a very important item), and need to be slotted in at an appropriate point in a service. The question that should be uppermost in the notice-giver's mind is 'What do I want to see as an end-result of this notice?' The notice should be written and presented with this in mind.

The more visual and dramatic a notice is, the more impact it will make, and the more it will be remembered. Therefore, visual aids, an overhead projector, drama and audio-visuals should be used wherever possible.

One to one

When all is said and done, the most effective form of communication is by a personal approach. Not only is this more likely to produce a response, but it is also possible to deal with any misunderstandings on the spot. It is very useful to identify people in the church who are in a key position to pass on information, or who have influence within certain groupings. If those people are enthusiastic and informed, they will encourage others.

EFFECTIVE COMMUNICATION

One danger in any church is that there will be too many notices. The church leaders need to determine the relative importance of notices and the most suitable way to present them. Sometimes a notice in a news-sheet would be better in the newsletter or as a general letter. Use the appropriate method, and use it sparingly. If something is very important, use several different methods to publicize it to the best effect. You will need to plan this carefully. The following example will illustrate this.

Recently our church embarked on training in evangelism using the *Person to Person* video-based training course. We wanted as many people as possible to take part, but the thought of 'training' and 'evangelism' produced reservations in the minds of many church members. As a result, a small group of key people met to preview the material, and two of them were given the task of promoting the venture. The course was to be used mainly in house groups, so we decided on a strategy for convincing the house group leaders, house group members and then other church members of the value of the course. Our first stage was to draw up an information leaflet about the 'why and how' of the course. This was attractively but cheaply produced. Members of the co-ordinating group then arranged visits to each house group leader to explain the contents and the practical details of the course, leaving a copy of the leaflet with them. The positive aspects of the course were emphasized, and any queries were answered. Now that house group leaders were in possession of the facts, they were better equipped to inform their groups. There was an encouraging response as people's worries and fears were expressed and answered.

The next stage was to encourage church members not normally involved in housegroups to get involved. This was done through (1) a colourful display on a large notice-board in the church; (2) an article in the church newsletter a week later; (3) a special announcement in the church services on the following Sunday. House group leaders made a special effort to invite sporadic attenders to join the course. Preachers made a point of mentioning the value of such training in their sermons. Further snippets were placed in subsequent issues of the newsletter. As a result there was a significant increase in normal house group attendance, for the first *Person to Person* sessions.

We can see from this example how several different forms of communication were used to keep people informed of what was going on, and to encourage them to take part. Such an approach needs careful planning, but it is very worthwhile.

Communication is hard work, but it is vital if people are to have enough information to pray specifically and effectively, and if the whole of the church is to be involved in an activity. It is one of the keys to uniting people in our evangelistic efforts, so that individuals are no longer beavering away in their own little corner, fragmenting the outreach of the church. Instead there will be a cohesive and co-ordinated approach that will be more likely to have a real impact on the community.

| NOTES |

1. For further information and advice refer to Administry. See Appendix 4 for address.

2. Churches can make use of special packages for photocopier rental. The Churches Purchasing Scheme can provide further information. See Appendix 4.

| SUMMARY |

● Involving the whole church in evangelism should be a major priority.

● Unity of effort is a key to effective evangelism.

● We need to be aware of the evangelistic potential of regular activities.

● Evangelism in the church should be co-ordinated by a specially chosen individual or small group.

● We should avoid:

□ activities working at cross purposes,

□ overworking key people.

● The whole church should be kept informed of evangelistic activities through the effective use of:

□ notice-boards,

□ church magazines,

□ news-sheets and letters,

□ church notices,

□ personal approaches.

● The aim of this information is to encourage:

□ prayer,

□ involvement.

| ACTION SHEET 5 |

EXERCISE 1

25 MINUTES – Draw up a list of every church activity/organization/ meeting. In groups use the criteria on page 92 and assess:

□ Has the activity been evangelistic in the past? Have people come into the orbit of the church through this activity? Have people become Christians through it?

□ Does it have the potential for being evangelistic? Would it be likely that non-Christians could involve themselves in the activity? Is it feasible to communicate the gospel either through informal conversation or through the activity itself – ie, is there opportunity for evangelistic input?

EXERCISE 2

25 MINUTES – Organize a 'gifts and abilities survey' amongst the church membership. In its simplest form this means asking individuals to list various tasks they do within the life of the church, or connected with their faith in a more general sense. Next to this, list the skills and

abilities that individuals have, or the things they would like to do. This is best done in very small groups, so that people are discouraged from being too modest or unrealistic about their abilities.

Begin by doing a survey amongst the members of this group. Divide into groups of four, and work round each person in turn. Put two groups together in order for members of the other group to add their comments and advise on the accuracy of the assessment of gifts. Again, this needs to be done in a spirit of love and encouragement, and yet honesty and accuracy need to prevail.

This kind of question – what are your gifts and abilities? – is often hard to answer. There are questionnaires produced, such as CWR's *Discovering your Spiritual Gifts*, which can help individuals take stock of their abilities. However, they can be very limited in scope, failing to assess people's natural

abilities, for example. This could be done by discovering what abilities people use in their normal work, eg communication skills, household budgeting, creative techniques, etc. All these can be used in the church's work of evangelism.

When the information has been collated for the church as a whole, the leaders can see:

☐ where people are involved in too many activities,

☐ where people are playing very little part in church life,

☐ where people are involved in activities which do not make use of their main gifts.

This is useful for the life of the church in general, but it can also be used to see how people could be actively involved in the various evangelistic activities and events. Individuals who are 'hiding their light under a bushel' may soon find their talents being used for the glory of God!

GET IT TOGETHER
PLANNING EVENTS AND MISSIONS

If you fail to plan, you plan to fail! Planning is essential for any form of mission activity. We can see evidence of short-term and long-term planning and strategy in the Bible. Jesus organized the disciples into pairs and gave them instructions for their task. Jesus' instructions for the evangelization of the world followed a basic strategy of beginning in Jerusalem, working into the surrounding country and then expanding to reach the whole of the world. Paul planned his missionary journeys – in each province he visited, he concentrated his evangelism on the capital city; his long-term goal was to reach Rome; the vision of the man from Macedonia persuaded him to change his *plans*.

THE PURPOSE OF PLANNING

There are several advantages in forward planning:

1. **It saves time**. If we did not take the trouble to plan, the ensuing chaos would ensure much wasted time. We would probably need several attempts to get everything right.

2. **It avoids duplication**. A little fact-finding will enable you to discover whether anyone else has similar intentions. There are few things more sickening than discovering that someone in the same town, or even in the same church, has planned a similar event.

3. **It allows mistakes**. It is far better to fail on paper than to fail in practice. Thinking through plans in advance increases the

chance of spotting pitfalls and problem areas before it is too late to avoid them.

4. It encourages flexibility. Some people imagine that planning is a very rigid process – plans must be followed according to the letter. Planning ahead can be very flexible. By thinking through the alternative approaches to achieving your objective, you will be able to make contingency plans which can be put into effect should the chosen course of action fail to work. Even at a late stage in the proceedings it is possible to change tracks provided you have prepared for such an eventuality.

5. It is a statement of faith. One of the arguments against planning is that it is 'unspiritual'. As we have already seen, planning is a biblical principle: Jesus points out the need for planning in the parables, and the Old Testament proverbs praise those who plan ahead. When we state our aims and objectives for evangelism we are stating in faith what we believe can be achieved with God's help.

6. It enables an accurate assessment to be made. If we have planned our strategy, we have a measure by which we can assess the success of our evangelistic efforts. In planning, we already have an idea of what we would like to see as a result of our activity. The more we plan, the more accurate our idea of what can be achieved will be, hence our objectives will become even more realistic.

7. It enables us to communicate our aims more effectively. We will have a precise idea of what is involved in our efforts, and what we are trying to achieve. This will help us to be succinct as we inform others in our church and nearby what will be happening. It will also help people to pray with clarity and understanding.

Planning can take place on several different levels: in the long and short term, in detail and in outline. In planning for evangelism we must be concerned with specific events and activities (see chapter 8), but also with a strategy for outreach over several years. This chapter is particularly concerned with the latter.

PLANNING A STRATEGY

We need to think in terms of a strategy that will give us aims and
objectives over the long term, so that we can avoid the 'What shall
we do this year?' syndrome. With a long-term strategy, we can
channel our resources and energies into a small number of areas. If
they prove fruitful, we will be satisfied. If they do not, we will at least
know that we have made a thorough effort to communicate the Good
News of Jesus in a particular way, or to a particular set of people.
We can then feel at peace about concentrating on a different set of
people, or using a different approach.

As a starting point to planning a strategy, we need to assess four
things: the needs of the area; the resources available; the
effort/achievement ratio; and, most importantly, what we feel God is
saying to us.

THE NEEDS OF THE AREA

In chapter 4 we looked at who we should be trying to reach with the
gospel, and how we can assess the needs of an area. Once we have
this information we can feed it into our strategy planning. It would
be a waste of time planning a mission to children and young people
on an estate consisting almost entirely of retirement homes. We
would be foolish to set up a drop-in centre for the unemployed in
a town where the numbers on the dole are less than one per cent of
the adult population. The needs of the community, and the groups
of people who live there, will shape our planning, and provide our
terms of reference.

We also need to assess the needs of our church. The emphasis
in Paul's letters is on 'building up the church', not just in numbers,
but in faith. One church may find that its members' faith is stretched
by taking part in door-to-door visiting, since it involves them in
situations where they have to share their faith, and give a reason for
their beliefs. Christians who are already strong in their faith could
work with new Christians who are enthusiastic but lack experience.
Another church may have a dearth of young people. A strategy for
youth evangelism may be necessary in their case. As a general rule
I would advise starting from a position of strength, rather than

weakness. By this I mean capitalizing on the resources you already have, rather than plunging into a venture in which you have no expertise. For example, if you have several elderly people, start a lunch club for the retired. If you have more young people, a youth club may be appropriate. The effects of failure in an area where you are strong would be less demoralizing than in an area of weakness.

THE AVAILABLE RESOURCES

We need to work within our own resources, and the resources that we believe God will provide. To do this, we must be aware of the resources that we have available. Key resources include:

People God uses people. He uses you and me in evangelism. People are the most valuable commodity that we have available for evangelism. We saw in chapter 2 the importance of personal witness, and in chapter 5 the need to involve as many people as possible in our outreach. However, it is extremely important that we do not overstretch people. Exhaustion and over-work should never be underestimated. There is a tendency among Christians to run themselves into the ground 'for the Lord', and look on their exhaustion as a mark of spirituality. This is madness. I am convinced that God would far rather have a church full of people close to their best, than a church full of physical and emotional wrecks.

We need to ensure that key people are not being used in too many areas, but that everyone has a part to play. We need to be aware of how many people will be needed to take responsibility for the planning and preparation of evangelism over the long term, as well as for individual events. The manpower we have available will be a guide as to how much evangelism we can undertake. We should not expect God to provide our church with extra people – except as a *result* of our evangelism. If someone comes to us from another church, then that church is deprived of their gifts and abilities. There are people with specialist skills such as evangelists, musicians, drama groups, trainers, etc. We can invite such people to take part in our evangelism, but the bulk of the work should always lie with the indigenous membership. This will be much more helpful in the long term.

Premises Sometimes we will be using the homes of church members for evangelism, but for special events we shall probably need a hall, or a large room. We need to examine our own premises, and ask the following questions:

● How large is the venue? How many people can be comfortably seated?

● For what types of event would it be suitable? Are the acoustics suitable for live music? Do we have a Performing Rights licence? Is there a blackout for films? Are there kitchen facilities for preparing food? etc.

● How convenient are the premises? Are they within easy reach of the people who will be invited? Will our activities cause unreasonable disturbance for the neighbours?

Once we have an accurate idea of the uses we can make of our own premises we can look at other possible venues in the area. We need to assess their precise suitability, and discover whether they are available for hire, and if so, with how much notice and at what cost.

Equipment It is very useful to have a list of equipment and facilities available for the church to use. This can range from the more basic such as chairs (are there enough for a particular event?) to the technical, such as PA equipment. Keeping a list will give some idea of how easy it will be to stage certain events, and also the sort of budget which will be needed if any equipment (especially the more technical) has to be hired.

Finance In some churches this is the first consideration; in others it's the last. Money is still a touchy issue in church circles, and yet in terms of a programme of outreach it is limiting factor. Churches need to be realistic and yet bold. We need to discover the very fine dividing line between 'It doesn't matter how expensive it is, God will provide' and 'It's out of the question. There's no way we can raise any more money than we do now.' I firmly believe that a church should budget a large proportion of its expenditure for evangelism. Failure to do so is a statement that it considers outreach to be unimportant. Another advantage of formulating a programme of evangelism is that it can be costed in advance.

Finance is needed in three main areas: premises and equipment, personnel, and publicity.

The first – the cost of premises and equipment – could include hire and purchase. For some pieces of equipment you may want to compare the two. In addition to hiring premises, you may need to pay for a Performing Rights licence, if live or recorded music is to be used.

Personnel who come in a professional capacity to take part in activities will need to be paid. Some evangelists and artistes will have a set fee which may be inclusive or exclusive of expenses; others will leave it entirely in the hands of the organizers. I would plead for a generous and realistic attitude on the part of organizers, especially if the person in question depends on such payments to earn his living. One guideline would be to work out a day's pay for an average salary, currently in the £40–£60 bracket, and pay accordingly. Preparation time should also be included in the payment.

The third cost is publicity. If an event is worth doing, it is worth telling people about it. In chapter 10 we will look at different methods of publicizing events, and how to do it economically. However, we need to maintain a minimum standard of quality and must be prepared to pay for it.

The amount of money that we make available will affect the number, quality and effectiveness of the activities that we plan. We need to work within our financial means, and yet we must not forget that we have a generous God who longs to see people reached with the gospel. Therefore we must not be afraid of stretching our faith in the area of finance and going beyond our natural expectations. This will need a commitment from people to find the necessary money. It's amazing how people are galvanized into action when they realize that this is their responsibility.

Now we know the resources we have available, and the amount for which we can trust God

THE EFFORT/ACHIEVEMENT RATIO

Sometimes we put an incredible amount of effort into an activity for little result. This is particularly dangerous if we are running people into the ground and finding ourselves in financial difficulty for the sake of putting on a programme. This may be because we want to put on something spectacular, such as a mission involving large events. Common sense tells us that it is far better to encourage personal witness, and arrange a series of small and informal bi-monthly activities than to arrange a one-week mega-mission with all kinds of speakers and artistes taking part. This is certainly the case if (i) there is no regular programme of outreach taking place, or (ii) the active membership of the church is small, or (iii) there is a steady stream of people committing their lives to following Christ without any major events.

We need to look at major projects in terms of their likely effect on our own resources, on our participants, and on the people we are trying to reach. Major projects should only take place if we know that God is guiding us to embark on them. Even then, they should be implemented on the firm foundation of day-to-day witness, a programme of outreach, and the resources and people capable of co-ordinating the event.

DISCERNING GOD'S WILL

We know God's heart in this matter: he longs that all people should be saved. Therefore a church that is not evangelizing is ignoring the will of God. However, we also need God's direction for our evangelism. What areas should we be concentrating on? God wants us to use our minds and our common sense, and yet he wants us to know his approval and to be open to his direct guidance. This can only be done prayerfully. Thus the act of praying should be second in our list of priorities.

'Second?' you may be asking. 'You said prayer came first!' Prayer is a two-way process, and the first priority is to *listen*. It is little use talking to God about our plans, if we fail to listen to him. After all, whose plans are most likely to succeed?

Prayer to discern God's will should permeate the whole process of planning a strategy. At all stages, commit the planning to God and listen for his confirmation or otherwise. As you discover the needs of your area you may hear God stressing one aspect in particular. As you look at your resources you will see that they are better suited to meeting some needs than others. With insight, you will be aware of what is achievable with those resources.

You will be amazed at how your strategy will crystallize into something that is within your capabilities, uses your resources efficiently, meets specific needs and, most importantly, is perceived as being what God wants.

GET IT TOGETHER –
AN EXAMPLE OF PLANNING

The best way to describe planning is by means of an example. Let us look at the fictional town of Oldtown. Most churches there have ageing congregations and make little impact on the new estates which have effectively doubled the population of the town, and whose inhabitants are mainly young married couples.

In our church there is a strong nucleus of young people. In addition, we have, over recent years, had contact with several young couples. Many of them were married in the church; some of these, and others, make use of the mother and toddler group.

One of the advantages of having a nucleus of young people earning relatively good salaries is that the church has an adequate income, and good prospects of raising enough extra money to finance a series of events. Another is that the workload of such a programme could be spread fairly evenly.

These were the features that stood out from our survey of needs in the area and resources in the church. They led us to decide on the strategy of reaching people in their twenties, particularly married couples, in Oldtown with the gospel. I hasten to point out that we should be wary of excluding singles from such a programme, but for the sake of describing the planning process I have restricted this example to married couples.

SETTING AIMS AND OBJECTIVES

Now that we have established our strategy we are in a position to begin planning. Our process for planning is summarized in figure 6a. We set our aims and objectives and then examine the various approaches we could use to meet them. Next we select the approach

EFFECTIVE PLANNING

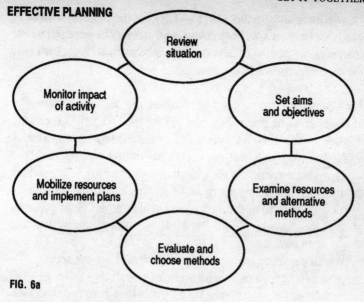

FIG. 6a

that we will use, put it into action, and afterwards evaluate how successful we have been.

Setting aims and objectives will help us to see how we can achieve something that is worthwhile rather than just putting on an event and hoping for the best. Aims and objectives are described differently by different writers and trainers. Some call them by other names such as targets and goals, and to add to the confusion objectives will be called targets by one writer and goals by another! The following are the definitions I am using:

Aims are statements which, although they give a direction, are not quantifiable in an absolute sense. Hence 'to present the gospel to friends of the young married couples in the church' would be classified as an aim.

Objectives are means towards the aims. They are more specific, and must be quantifiable. They need to be questioned very critically. For example, are they realistic? Are they practical?

Targets provide a means of measuring our progress in achieving our objectives. They are very specific, and therefore very achievable. A target is a refined objective.

Methods are specific activities. They are the concrete ways in which we can reach our objectives. After setting our aims and objectives, we can then assess the alternative methods before selecting the most appropriate in our situation.

Let's continue with our example. We have decided on the strategy of reaching young married couples in Oldtown. We need to set aims to work towards this. We can do this by highlighting three groups of young married people that our church has contact with. First, those who have been married in the church over the past five years, second, the friends of the young marrieds within the church, and third, the couples represented at the mother and toddler group. Reaching any or all of these groups will work towards our strategy, and is therefore shown as an aim.

Within our aims, we need to set objectives. Take the second group of people we aim to reach with the gospel: the friends of young marrieds in the church. We may decide to have two objectives to work towards this aim. One is to train the young marrieds in the church in personal witnessing, and the second is to arrange a series of events of a predominantly social nature, but which also contain an introduction to the Christian message.

We can now set ourselves a target for each of these objectives. For the first, our target is to train sixteen out of the twenty-six couples in the church. For the second, our target is that fifty contacts should have attended at least one event. Another target will stretch our faith, but it provides a specific objective to pray towards: two couples to become Christians within the year. These targets act as an incentive, and will add to the motivation of all involved.

Having decided what achieving our objectives will involve, we need to set out the alternative methods of working towards them and look at the resources needed. One of the ways we could achieve objective 2 (holding social events with a Christian content) would be to organize a series of dinners and cabarets at the church hall. We have the facilities – a spacious and well equipped kitchen, a superb caterer, plenty of chairs, and access to tables at a nearby church. Another method is to arrange social outings, such as ten-pin bowling at a nearby alley. This may prove to be a better start since it is more socially orientated, and allows relationships to be established. Gradually we have built up a picture of what we want to achieve and different methods for achieving it. (See figure 6b on page 114.) Having selected our methods, we can then implement our plans.

(This style of planning is also useful for determining the purpose of activities already in existence. We simply start at the bottom of a sheet of paper by writing down the method, and then work out its objectives and what aim they have in mind. This will help us to assess its usefulness in the church programme: does it have a worthwhile and relevant aim?)

SHARED AIMS

'Whose aims?' is a very important question. An organization of any description is less likely to achieve its aims and objectives unless they are shared by all involved. In practical terms this means a total commitment from the co-ordinating group and/or leadership. It also means spending time helping members of the congregation understand what you are trying to achieve and why. You will have succeeded when you score an 'owned goal' – ie people own the aims and objectives for themselves. Instead of being the leadership's aims they are 'our aims'.

This can be achieved by involving people in discussing plans, asking them for their comments and paying attention to the feedback. Involving them in praying, not just after plans have been made but while they are being formulated, will also lead to a sense of shared aims. The more that people feel involved in the planning, the harder they will work to achieve the objectives.

FORMULATING A PROGRAMME OF OUTREACH

An isolated evangelistic event will probably achieve very little. If on the other hand it is part of a programme of evangelism there will be much greater scope for achieving something of lasting value. It will build on what has gone before, and prepare for what is to come. It

EXAMPLE OF PLANNING

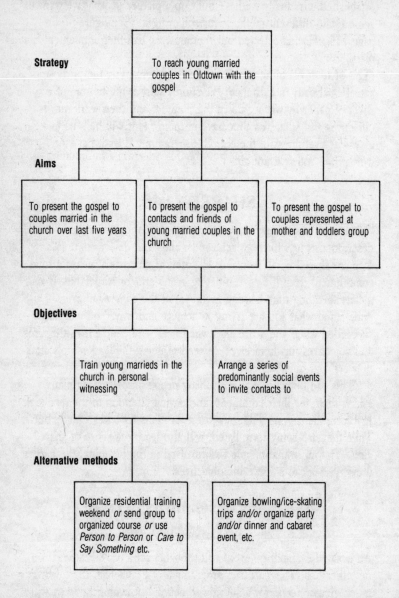

Strategy

To reach young married couples in Oldtown with the gospel

Aims

To present the gospel to couples married in the church over last five years

To present the gospel to contacts and friends of young married couples in the church

To present the gospel to couples represented at mother and toddlers group

Objectives

Train young marrieds in the church in personal witnessing

Arrange a series of predominantly social events to invite contacts to

Alternative methods

Organize residential training weekend *or* send group to organized course *or* use *Person to Person* or *Care to Say Something* etc.

Organize bowling/ice-skating trips *and/or* organize party *and/or* dinner and cabaret event, etc.

FIG. 6b

will provide another occasion for people to be challenged with the gospel of Christ. How can we construct an effective programme?

Firstly, we need that foundation of day-to-day witnessing. Secondly we need to take into account the evangelistic aspects of current activities. Thirdly, we need to take into consideration the aims and objectives that have been formulated. As we saw in chapter 3, conversion is a process, involving various stages. A programme should allow people to be introduced to the gospel and then take them through the stage of understanding to commitment and discipleship. Hence, initial activities should assume little if any knowledge of Christianity. They should concentrate on building relationships. The most effective evangelism will normally occur over a length of time.

Any programme should be spaced out so that the diary does not become too crowded, but there should not be too large a gap between activities. Common sense is as good a guide as any, and judgment will improve with experience. Events differ in their evangelistic intensity; their size in terms of organization and impact; and their potential for drawing in people. We need to be aware of the differences. Some events, such as concerts, are obviously high in profile and in impact. Other events such as barbecues and discussion groups are low-key events. A balanced programme will space out high-profile events, liberally interspersing them with low key events. This is best pictured as a series of peaks and troughs – see figure 6c on page 116. It will carry more momentum than the other patterns illustrated where there is a big bang at the beginning or end of the pattern, but little to sustain interest over a lengthy period. An example of a well-balanced programme is shown in figure 6d. Notice the peaks and troughs which occur over the year.

PLANNING A MISSION

I have tried during the preceding chapters to show that evangelism is much more than putting on a mission. Indeed, I would actively discourage a church from organizing a major outreach without getting its act together in terms of personal witness, a programme of evangelism and facilities for follow-up. A mission works best in this

A BALANCED PROGRAMME

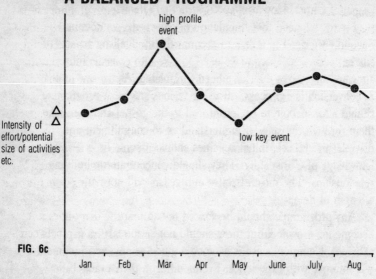

high profile event

Intensity of effort/potential size of activities etc.

low key event

FIG. 6c

Jan   Feb   Mar   Apr   May   June   July   Aug

EXAMPLE OF A BALANCED PROGRAMME

Programme for young marrieds outreach

January	Ice skating trip
February	Bowling trip
March	Dinner and cabaret with musician*
April	'Golden Oldies' record evening
May	Trip to production of *Godspell*
June	Cricket match: husbands vs wives
July	Barbecue with speaker
August	Outing to Cambridge with punting
September	Moving feast (different courses at different houses)
October	Video evening
November	Dinner and cabaret with drama group and speaker*
December	Party

*Clear presentation of gospel mesage

FIG. 6d

context because it should be a time of reaping following on from a time of sowing. It is true that God can do the sowing, but more often than not he chooses us to be involved in that process. We are deluding ourselves if we assume that a mission will automatically be successful, but have given no thought to sowing the seed.

Missions can be very exciting times, but unless we are prepared to get our hands dirty, and to spend the time in preparation they can be a lot of excitement about nothing. I speak from experience. The most effective missions are those in which Christians are on the ground, building relationships, providing a natural point of contact. If your church is considering organizing a mission, suggest that it takes place over two years with a focal point of a high-profile week or so, somewhere in the middle of that programme. This is far more realistic.

A mission needs to fit in with the aims and objectives that the church has set for its outreach. Avoid the temptation of having too large a target. It is better to have a modest target that can be reached than to make an insignificant gesture towards a grandiose scheme. The target needs to be within the resources of the church otherwise the strain could be counter-productive. The practicalities of organizing mission events and activities will be covered in chapter 8.

EVALUATING YOUR PROGRESS

Evaluation is as important as planning. Part of the point of planning is to work towards a goal. We can measure our success by evaluating our achievements. In this way we will benefit from our mistakes and learn lessons that will be valuable in planning the next stage of our outreach.

The most basic question to ask is, 'Did we achieve our objectives?' If the answer is yes, then our planning was successful – although we should be aware of any unforeseen factors that helped our plans. If the answer is no, then we should ask a few more questions, to determine what went wrong. Was our planning unrealistic? Did we fail to take certain factors into account? Was there a breakdown in communications? Did everyone carry out their tasks as directed? Were we wrong in any of our basic assumptions?

These kinds of questions help us move on to another phase of outreach better equipped. Evaluation should always be programmed in right at the start, otherwise it would be easy to forget about it. It is a good idea to hold regular evaluations during a programme; this makes it easier to make alterations that would benefit that particular programme. To be accurate, evaluation needs feedback from the organizers, the Christians actively involved in the activities, those who attend, and, if possible, outside observers.

In part 2 of this book I have dealt with the preparation necessary before embarking on evangelism. The final part of the book deals with the nuts and bolts of evangelistic events and missions.

| SUMMARY |

● Planning is vital to evangelism. Planning:

   □ saves time,

   □ avoids duplication,

   □ avoids mistakes,

   □ encourages flexibility,

   □ is a statement of faith,

   □ enables evaluation,

   □ encourages communication of aims.

● Preparations for planning include:

   □ assessing the needs of the area,

   □ assessing the available resources: people; premises; equipment; finance,

   □ assessing the effort/achievement ratio,

   □ discerning God's will.

● Set realistic aims and objectives shared by all involved.

● Formulate a balanced and purposeful programme.

● Missions should be planned against a background of ongoing, personal witness and a programme of evangelistic activities.

● Evaluate your progress regularly.

| ACTION SHEET 6 |

EXERCISE 1

This exercise is designed to encourage people to think in terms of aims and objectives, and it has a very useful side effect since it will help evaluate the current activities of the church.

15 MINUTES – Each group of three or four is asked to write down the aims and objectives of a particular church activity or meeting. Thus on a chart, the activity is written at the bottom as a method, and then its aims and objectives are decided upon.

EXAMPLE

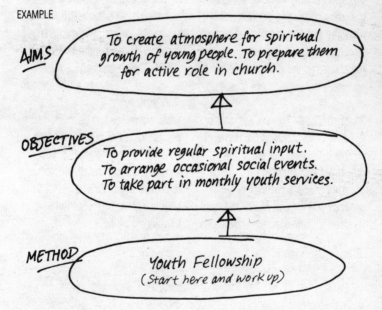

AIMS — To create atmosphere for spiritual growth of young people. To prepare them for active role in church.

OBJECTIVES — To provide regular spiritual input. To arrange occasional social events. To take part in monthly youth services.

METHOD — Youth Fellowship (Start here and work up)

Be critical about the validity of the aims and objectives, and ask to what degree the activity is achieving them. In this example, if I were a leader of the church, I would question the underlying assmption that young people cannot already have an active role in the church.

10 MINUTES – After each group has finished show conclusions to the whole group for comment.

One interesting expansion of this is to ask those responsible for particular activities to go through the same process. A comparison between their conclusions and those of other church members will shown any disparity between the two views.

If they coincide, it is a clear indicator that the church membership is pulling in the same direction.

EXERCISE 2

Using the same groups as in the first exercise, give each group an evangelistic aim. This might result from the findings of Action Sheet 4. The groups now have to work out their objectives and methods of fulfilling that aim, and to set realistic targets. After completing this part of the task, pair the groups together to comment on each others' results.

20 MINUTES – The second part of the task is to plan a programme of activities to meet the aims and objectives.

This process will not only produce some good ideas that can be used in outreach, but it will also help members to understand that events are not aimless, isolated activities, but that they are working towards a goal.

20 MINUTES – Now ask the groups to dream a little, and to describe briefly three possible outcomes to their programme.

□ The most optimistic (eg 200 attend, 50 become Christians).
□ The most pessimistic (eg only 12 attend the event).
□ The most likely (eg 100 attend, 6 express an interest in Christianity).

What plans need to be made to cater for this range of outcomes? This will help you to plan ahead. It will certainly centre your thoughts on follow-up arrangements, but you should not restrict your thinking to this aspect alone.

PART

3

PRACTICALITIES

CHAPTER SEVEN

'... AND MAKE DISCIPLES'

FOLLOW-UP

Tragedy struck my family a few years ago when my sister's first child was still-born. There was much pain and hurt, especially for the parents, who have never fully recovered from the experience.

Just as the joy that surrounds someone becoming a Christian is similar to that accompanying the birth of a baby, so there is grief when someone's Christian commitment lapses within a few days of their initial decision. God's love for those who have been 'born again' is that of a father for his child, and his feelings when that new life doesn't develop into maturity must be similar.

The tragedy is that in many cases the termination of spiritual life could be avoided if only the church was more aware of how to care for and nurture new Christians. The discipling of those who are new in the faith must be a priority in our evangelism. Even if all our plans for outreach are successful, they will come to nothing unless our follow-up in terms of discipling and nurturing is right. We need to understand what is meant by 'discipling' and 'nurture', and there is no better place to look than the Bible.

THE BIBLICAL PATTERN
JESUS AND HIS DISCIPLES
The disciples were instrumental in the founding of the church. Their achievement was largely the result of the training they had been given by Jesus during his earthly ministry. That training did not take place in a classroom, nor even in a congregational setting, but through a close-knit personal relationship that Jesus developed with the twelve men who responded to his call to follow him.

Jesus shared his life with them. He was with them day and night, he ate with them, he talked with them, he let them see him in moments of glory and of weakness. Jesus showed his disciples how to live. He did the things that he expected them to do, so that they would model their lives on his. Before he sent his disciples out in pairs, he not only gave them instructions, he had already shown them how to minister. They were not always successful in following his example, but even their failures were used as lessons.

With the power of the Holy Spirit, this training enabled the disciples to establish the church. Even the religious and political authorities who opposed them noticed that the difference in the lives of these uneducated fishermen was caused by the fact that they had been with Jesus.

PAUL'S EXAMPLE
Paul also had disciples. He took fellow Christians with him on his journeys and they grew in their faith through working and travelling with him. The list includes Silas, Barnabas, John Mark, Timothy and Luke. They were all at different stages in their Christian life, but each benefitted from their time with Paul.

Paul sums up the theory of discipling in 1 Corinthians 11:1, 'Follow my example, as I follow the example of Christ.' Paul describes how, in Thessalonica, '. . . we lived among you for your sake. You became imitators of us and of the Lord. . . . And so you became a model to all the believers in Macedonia and Achaia' (1 Thessalonians 1:5–7).

OLD TESTAMENT PRECEDENTS

Discipling is not restricted to the New Testament. We can see a similar pattern amongst the Old Testament prophets. The most obvious example is that of Elijah and Elisha. Elijah trained his successor to follow in his footsteps, in the same way that a craftsman trains an apprentice in his skills.

APPRENTICESHIP FOR LIFE

The biblical pattern for discipleship is one of apprenticeship for life. It is a learning process, which concentrates on practice rather than theory. In his film and book series *Jesus, Then and Now*, David Watson summarizes the process of discipling into four stages. Firstly, you watch while I do; secondly, we do it together; thirdly, you do while I watch; fourthly, you do it on your own. This is how Christianity was passed on in the early church.

Discipling is an aspect of church life that has by and large been lost to the modern church, and yet it is essential if we are to see lives changed radically. Such discipleship is costly in terms of time and commitment. It does occur, often without people realizing, but not on the scale of the early church.

Even if we cannot make such a commitment, we must at least ensure that there is some form of initial discipling of new Christians. They have entered a new world, which may seem very strange. There will be new experiences, and also new skills to learn that will help them to make the most of this new life. Like babies they need much care and attention.

No-one in their right mind welcomes a newborn baby with the words, 'Hello, glad to see you've arrived. We're off for a few days, so here's a can opener and there's the fridge!' During the first few years of life, babies need almost constant attention. They undergo the greatest physical change that they will ever face. They are incredibly vulnerable and need protection. They need to learn how to survive in the world.

It is much the same for new Christians. How will they know how to live as Christians unless someone shows them? How will they know what to believe, unless someone helps them? All too often we see people become Christians, and we wrongly assume that they understand everything they need to know. It is our responsibility as a church to nurture new believers, and the way that this is done will influence them for the rest of their lives.

ONE-TO-ONE DISCIPLING

One-to-one discipling occurs when a new Christian meets regularly with a mature believer to discover more about their new-found faith. This resembles the Pauline model. It enables a strong relationship to be built between the discipler and the new Christian. It enables the new believer to be more open about his or her needs, doubts and questions in a way that would be difficult in a group. The discipler is in a better position to find out what stage the new Christian has reached; they can go back over ground where there is doubt or misunderstanding. They can ensure that the new Christian really understands the basics of Christian belief and living. Meetings together can be more flexible, since only two people will be involved in making the arrangements.

One of the keys to success in one-to-one discipling is the matching of the two people. If their relationship is good, it will benefit the learning process. If it is bad, it could hinder the growth of the new Christian. They should be of the same sex so that romantic involvement doesn't get in the way. It helps if the two are of similar ages, and have some interests in common. Discipleship involves more than merely learning a set of facts or instructions; by being able to share in activities and talk about interests other than Christianity, the new Christian will see that faith affects the whole of life. The key to Jesus' discipling was that he shared the whole of his life with his followers. Even if we are not prepared to go as far as this, it is still very important that new Christians have the opportunity to glimpse how faith affects a believer's life.

NURTURE GROUPS

The other main method of early discipling is through a nurture group. One or more mature Christians meet with a larger number of new Christians on a regular basis to help them learn about the Christian life, faith and community. The communal aspect is the main feature of a nurture group. It introduces new Christians to the corporate aspect of being a Christian and helps to prepare them for church life.

Nurture groups allow members to become familiar with the caring and sharing aspect of the church, as well as with corporate worship such as praying and reading the Bible in public. For those who have come to a Christian commitment outside the church, it can be a vital stage in their integration into the life of the church. It provides a similar function for a new Christian as a nursery does for a young child.

We must beware of taking the analogy too far. We should not fall into the trap of treating new Christians as children, for example, or of adopting a patronizing attitude. Some new Christians will be far more intelligent than we are. Some will have a quicker grasp of spiritual truths than we will ever have. You may be surprised to discover how much they know and understand about Christianity! Or how little!

In any group, even in the church, there is a risk that progress will be affected by group dynamics. The nurture group leader will need some basic instruction on how to lead a group, and how to deal with people in this situation. The leader's guide in *Caring for New Christians* (see Resources List, Appendix 3) is particularly useful in this respect.

One disadvantage of a nurture group is that it is harder to get to know group members than in the one-to-one situation. That is why it is important to develop individual relationships with each group member outside the group meeting. An ideal arrangement will incorporate both one-to-one discipling and a nurture group.

GETTING ORGANIZED

DISCIPLESHIP CO-ORDINATOR

Someone will need to co-ordinate the discipling in a church – to decide on the methods, choose the materials, and link up new Christians with disciplers. Very early in the process the co-ordinator will need to meet with the church leadership, to decide who should be a discipler.

QUALITIES OF A DISCIPLER
There are three qualities which are essential in a discipler. Firstly, to be strong in their own faith and show evidence of their maturity (this doesn't mean they should necessarily be old!). Secondly, they should be easy communicators, able to explain with clarity and honesty. Thirdly, they should be open in a responsible way: able to share their faith by allowing people to get to know them. Please note, you will rarely discover the ideal discipler, but each element should be evident, at least to some degree.

PRACTICAL ARRANGEMENTS
The discipleship co-ordinator will also need to be available to give advice on any of the following areas, though decisions will vary from situation to situation. Problems may arise from time to time, so the co-ordinator will need to step in decisively, but with sensitivity.

Where to meet
An informal setting is most conducive to building relationships. The discipler's house is best, unless there are likely to be frequent interruptions.

When to meet
Meetings need to be regular: weekly if possible. During the early stages, especially in the one-to-one situation, the new Christian benefits from frequent encouragement, so it is worth phoning them once or twice between meetings. Some people will need this more than others: the discipler will need to be sensitive to their differing needs. The start time should be mutually agreed, and sessions should not go on beyond an hour except at the instigation of the new Christian. In a group situation, it is very important to keep to time, especially where sensitivity to members' families is necessary.

How many meetings?
This will vary according to the situation, the people involved, and the material to be used. Courses that I have used vary between six and fifteen sessions. You may want to meet for much longer – following the biblical ideal of continual discipling. This needs mutual

agreement and must not obstruct the new Christian's integration into the church.

'... TEACHING THEM. ...'

The quality of the relationship between the new and the more mature Christian is important in any discipling situation. The aim of nurture is to help the new Christian to develop links within the church community, and to enable him or her to grasp the basics of the Christian faith. The basics which should be taught are as follows:

1. Christian Living. A new Christian needs help in developing his or her newfound relationship with God. It is not easy getting to know someone who is not with you physically – it needs Christ's representative (ie you) to play a part. Stress the importance of getting to know God through reading the Bible regularly, and spending time talking and listening to God through prayer. The discipler will need to show new Christians, especially those without a church background, how this can be done. He or she could even invite the new Christian to share in his private devotions (quiet time), to give them an insight and, if suitable, a pattern.

The need for commitment to a body of believers should also be emphasized. New Christians who are not familiar with church services may need to be taken along and helped through the service. We can be so familiar with worship that we forget how alien some of the things we do in church might seem to outsiders. This is true for traditional services (jumping from page to page in the Prayer Book can be very daunting) and for more informal worship (especially when it comes to the use of charismatic gifts). The discipler will need to put the new Christian's mind at rest by explaining what is happening and, later, why it happened.

Encourage new Christians to submit their behaviour and decisions to God. It is very difficult to give up lifelong habits such as swearing, or to let go of resentments that are rooted in history. Another important area is learning to resist temptation. Often only the power of the Holy Spirit can enable a person to change, but our task is to show clearly how we should be living as Christians.

2. Christian Beliefs. As Christians we never stop learning about our faith, and one of the church's major roles is to pass on Christ's teaching. However there are certain basics of the Christian faith which need to be grasped, understood, and then applied to the life of the new Christian.

Basic questions need to be answered: Who is God? How does he relate to the world? What is sin? What does it do? How did Jesus deal with sin? Why did he have to die? How can we be re-united with God? Where does the Holy Spirit fit into all of this? In our post-Christian society, there is much ignorance about Christian doctrines, and many new Christians will not have thought such things through thoroughly before making a commitment. A discipler will invariably discover that new Christians have many misconceptions that need to be corrected. Often materialism has had such a profound influence that people find difficulty in grasping spiritual truths.

These beliefs cannot be learnt by rote; they need to be understood. The way they are presented is therefore very important. Levels of understanding will vary considerably between people, and this also needs to be taken into account. Meeting together, whether on a one-to-one basis or in a group, should be like a voyage of discovery. Recent material specifically designed for use in discipling is geared to such an approach.

TOOLS FOR THE JOB

Details of all the following are given in the Resources List (Appendix 3).

Caring for New Christians was one of the first nurture group courses to be published commercially. A group meets for six sessions, and majors on the communal aspects of the Christian life. Although Bible study is central to each session, group members are encouraged to pray and worship together and this is a good introduction to active involvement in church life. Six training sessions for group leaders are also included covering the main areas of nurturing new Christians and leading a group. This in itself is very useful even if alternative material is used with group members.

LIFE: New Life with Jesus Christ is a fifteen-week course aimed at young people or non-intellectual adults. It comprises a folder with fifteen sheets, each covering a different topic. The sheets can be used in any order, although the recommended sequence is suitable for most situations. This allows a discipler to be flexible in responding to questions a new Christian may raise. The sheets are designed to enable the new Christian to work through them on their own, answering questions by looking up Bible references. The questions are not taxing, although some will find it difficult moving around the Bible. The discipler can go over the sheet when the two meet. This approach can work in both one-to-one and group situations.

For those who have been through higher education, *Think It Through* would probably be more suitable. This is a series of Bible studies which looks at the implications of certain Bible passages, and encourages application.

Young people will find *The Transformation Pack* or *Growing More Like Jesus* suited to their needs. *The Transformation Pack* consists of eight cards in a folder, each explaining one aspect of Christianity. It makes good use of illustrations, but in order to be used most effectively the discipler needs to have a good grasp of the theory of discipling. It can be used for most ability levels. *Growing More Like Jesus* is designed for use in groups, and is geared to young teenagers.

Such resources may not be suitable for your particular situation, but they could be used as a basis for developing your own material. *49 Steps*, for example, provides an exhaustive outline for a discipling course, and would make a good starting point.

AN OPPORTUNITY LOST?

One problem remains. Hundreds, perhaps thousands, of people who have been challenged to make a Christian commitment at a particular event or occasion simply have not been ready to make such a decision. Some will not have responded in any way, others may have made a response which appears to be a commitment, and yet within a short length of time will have drifted away.

The vast majority of people need time to consider carefully their decision to follow Christ. They also need sufficient information on which to base their decision. The more time and information they have, the more likely they are to make a commitment that will last for the rest of their lives.

It is vital, therefore, that we consider the question, 'What happens to those who respond to an evangelistic challenge, but decide that they are not yet ready to make a commitment?' By providing for such people, we can avoid the lost opportunity they might otherwise represent.

What is needed is a relaxed atmosphere, without any pressure being applied, in which interested people can learn more about the Christian faith and be given the opportunity to respond in their own way and in their own time. The Holy Spirit can work in this atmosphere just as well as anywhere else, and those involved will feel much more in control of their decision than in a large gathering where emotional pressure may be perceived.

OPEN-MINDED ENQUIRY

An excellent format for this approach is an enquirers' group. A small number of open-minded people meet in a group with a Christian to look at Christianity. It should provide an opportunity for beliefs and practices to be examined and questioned, without preconceptions or assumptions being made. This can be a very refreshing approach, not only for the enquirers but also for the group leader. Any hint of propaganda should be avoided in order for the group sessions to work well.

An enquirers' group needs to look at basic questions that would help a person to understand the essentials of being a Christian. It needs to deal with the central issues of faith. The person and work of Jesus should be fundamental in any course. Questions such as 'Who is Jesus?', 'Why did Jesus have to die?' and 'Is Jesus important today?' need to be considered. 'How can you become a Christian?' is also essential, but the questioning should not stop there. 'What is it like being Christian?' and 'How does the church fit in?' are equally valid and important questions. We need to be very open, and to discuss the disadvantages as well as the advantages of being a Christian. It may be necessary to cover other areas such as 'How can we know that there is a God?' and 'Can we trust the Bible?' At the heart of the enquiry is the basic question, 'How do you know it is real?' People are looking for something that is real. Any suspicion that the wool is being pulled over their eyes will make them very wary. Therefore we need to be totally open and honest. The choice of leader for such a group will be crucial.

ANY QUESTIONS?

Certain elements can be included to enhance this open-minded approach. Another Christian could be invited to a group session to answer questions from his or her own experience. This will shed further light on particular topics. They might, for example, speak for a few minutes on 'How Christianity has changed my life' or 'Why I am convinced that Christianity is true', and then answer any questions that group members wish to ask them. A series of different 'guests' will enable members to meet several different Christians and 'grill' them about their faith.

Another useful activity is to attend a church service. This is especially important if members of the group are not familiar with the church. They should not be there to participate in the service but rather to act as observers. Following the service, they should be given the opportunity to ask their group leader, or preferably one of the church leaders, questions about the service. They should be encouraged to discover why things are done in certain ways in order to break down the 'mystique' of religious services.

In both these suggestions, the open-minded approach needs to be maintained. The Christians may put forward their views strongly, but enquirers must be able to question them with no holds barred!

This approach is used in *Just Looking*, an enquirers' group course designed by John Allan (see list in Appendix 3). This is the first course to be designed specifically for open-minded enquiry. It is written for young people, mainly for sixth-formers and reasonably intelligent fourth and fifth years, but the principles apply to any age range. I would welcome similar material designed for other age groups and ability levels.

The best material that I have come across for non-literate young people, is *Weenies* written by Fran Morrison. *Weenies* begins as an enquirers' course but turns into discipleship material after several sessions. The basic idea behind the course is that many young people (indeed, many adults) find it easier to think in terms of pictures and images than in the abstract. Hence the character of God is shown by the passage from Isaiah 6, which pictures God in all his glory. The images are used to develop an understanding of the greatness of God. An extract from *Weenies* is included in Appendix 2.

ORIGINAL MATERIAL

There is plenty of scope for designing your own enquirers' group material. In fact, if you are dealing with adults, you will probably need to do so since there is so little suitable material available! The key is to think how you can best help enquiring minds to discover the truth of Christianity for themselves. *Just Looking* and *Weenies* will provide plenty of ideas for approaches and content. Evangelistic Bible studies (see chapter 3) can also be used. When designing material it is important to: keep meetings brief; allow plenty of opportunities for questions; provide plenty of information in easily digestible chunks; give room for group members to make their own decision in their own time.

Designing your own discipleship or enquirers' material will enable you to gear it to your particular church and the people with whom you are working. Several churches have already produced their own material.

THE BOTTOM LINE

If we fail to follow-up people who express an interest in Christianity, whether as an enquirer or as a new believer, we are disobeying Christ's command. It is not good enough merely to preach the Good News, we should be in the business of making disciples. We are involved in bringing people through this process of new birth, and that needs a lot of care and attention, and will involve both joy and heartache. It needs to be done with integrity and enthusiasm. Successful evangelism needs good follow-up. Without it all the time, effort and trouble is wasted.

| SUMMARY |

- Follow-up is vital if evangelism is to reach its goal.
- The biblical pattern for discipling is seen in the examples of Jesus, Paul, and Elijah. Biblical discipleship is apprenticeship for life.
- We must provide at least initial discipling in either one-to-one or nurture group format.
- Discipleship involves learning how to live and what to believe.

- Enquirers' groups should be provided for those who are not yet ready to commit their lives to Christ, but who are interested in finding out more.
- There is material available commercially, but original material can be prepared, and may be more suitable.

| ACTION SHEET 7 |

EXERCISE 1

5 MINUTES – Ask individuals to think over their Christian life, and to write down anything that has particularly helped them to grow in their faith. Lists might include people and/or experiences that were especially helpful.

10 MINUTES – Forming into groups of three or four, encourage people to share their lists with one another. This may bring to mind other factors that people will want to add to their list.

10 MINUTES – In the whole group discuss whether we can learn any lessons that would help us to understand the process of discipleship, and that can be applied in any arrangements for discipling new Christians.

EXERCISE 2

10 MINUTES – Individually compile two lists. The first list is of actions and behaviour that should be encouraged in the life of a new Christian (eg learning Bible verses, telling friends and family about their new faith, etc). The second list is of specific beliefs (doctrines) that need to be taught to a recent convert (eg why Jesus died, the 'fruit of the Spirit', etc). Use a table like that shown overleaf.

LAYOUT OF TABLE

In my opinion	PAIR – in our opinion	FOURSOME – in our opinion

10 MINUTES – In pairs compare lists, and discuss which eight items are the most important for a new Christian.

10 MINUTES – Pairing the pairs, so that now we have groups of four, compare these lists of eight and decide on the five most important in each of the two categories.

This exercise will help members to consider the essential aspects of Christian living and understanding that need to be grasped by new believers.

EXERCISE 3: ACTION EXTRA

A 'dummy run' of enquirers' and/or nurture groups can be very helpful – not only for those who intend to lead such groups, but also for people in the church who would be helped by going through a discipleship or enquirers' course. In most churches there will be people who have almost grown into membership, without really understanding what is involved in becoming a Christian. A 'dummy' nurture group would help them. There may also be people on the fringe of the church who have never got involved in church life to any real degree. A 'dummy' enquirers' group would challenge them to seriously consider their commitment. Other members of these dummy groups would be there simply to give the leader learning experience in their role.

WHEN THE RUBBER HITS THE ROAD

ORGANIZING EVANGELISTIC EVENTS, ACTIVITIES AND MISSIONS

This chapter is the kernel of the whole book. Other chapters are concerned with 'a little forethought' vital to the planning of outreach activities. This chapter deals with the actual organization of events, activities and missions. It draws together the various strands that have appeared elsewhere in the book and shows how everything ties together.

I shall look at organizing an event in some depth, before proceeding to other evangelistic activities and the high-profile, focal period of a mission. An event is a simple unit to deal with, and most of the principles and details will apply equally to the other cases.

ORGANIZING EVENTS

MAKING DECISIONS

Having spent time in prayer and planning (see chapter 6) you should be in a position where your evangelistic programme is now set for the next two or three years. You know the general direction in which you are heading and you know what you would like to achieve. You have a series of events and activities pencilled in, and now is the time to move from the theoretical to the practical. In the next few pages I shall take you through the stages of organizing an event. As an example I have chosen a dinner and cabaret since it involves several aspects that are common to other events. I shall mention variations that would apply in other circumstances as we go along.

Whatever event you are organizing, you should have clarified the purpose, style and content in your initial planning. In our example we are organizing a dinner and cabaret for young married couples in Oldtown. This event takes place in the second year of evangelistic activity, so many of the guests will have encountered the gospel message over the last few months. They are ready to be challenged to commit their lives to Christ so the evangelistic content will be more overt than in last year's events. The cabaret will be provided by a musician and a speaker.

MAKING THE BOOKINGS

Booking the artiste/speaker

We have drawn up a list of speakers and musicians who would probably be suitable, taking into account the people who will be invited. The list comes from one of the Christian Directories available in this country (see Resources List: Appendix 3) and from personal recommendations made by members of the group. We have decided who we would most like to invite, and initial contact will be made by one of the main organizers. At this stage it is best to use the telephone since the first question to ask any particular speaker or musician is whether they are available and willing to consider the booking. If not, they will say so immediately and long delays waiting for correspondence will be avoided. The other question to ask at this stage concerns finance. If they have a set fee which is beyond our budget then unless they are willing to negotiate we will have to move on to the next person on the list. It is best for both sides to know the other's position on finance as soon as possible, so that embarrassing situations do not arise later.

It is very important to see the artiste and speaker in action. This may be advisable before contacting them and is vital before a firm booking is made. This will provide an opportunity to check on the quality of their performance (is it suitable for the standard of our event?), and to see how they approach their task (is the speaker sensitive to his audience?). At some stage during the booking process it is a good idea to meet them face-to-face in order to discuss both sides' expectations. This is an absolute must for a mission or a series of evangelistic events involving the same artistes or speakers. It will help the organizers to ensure that they are on the same wavelength as the people who will be up-front.

After a provisional booking has been made there are several details that need sorting out. These are mostly practical:

● What kind of power supply is needed for equipment (number and type of sockets)?

● Will we need to hire PA or lights, or will the musician be bringing his own?

● If we do need to hire them, what specifications would suit the musician (power of PA; number of microphones; monitor speakers; type and power of lighting; colour of gels, etc)?

● Will we need to provide an operator for the lights/PA?

● How much setting-up/soundcheck time is needed?

● How many people will they be bringing with them?

● Will they need a meal before or after the event? What kind of meal?

● Will they require overnight accommodation? How many couples and singles/male or female?

● Do they need a map in order to find the venue?

● What is their time limit? You will need to decide how long you want them to speak or perform, but be flexible and open to suggestions. If they would prefer to operate differently, say performing two 20 minute sets rather than one 30 minute, it is better to negotiate at this stage.

If you have not done so, a written confirmation of the booking and the details already agreed should be sent, asking for a reply in writing. You can encourage co-operation by enclosing a stamped self-addressed envelope, and even a simple form to be completed and signed. Both organizer and artistes/speakers now know where they stand.

Booking the venue

This will apply even if it is on your own premises. It would be very humiliating to arrive on the night and discover that the Girls' Brigade are using the hall, refusing to allow any interruptions!

In our case, we have decided to go up-market and hire a suite at the local civic centre. Our first move is to contact the booking officer to enquire about availability, and to confirm what facilities will be provided. The question of whether to book the venue or the artistes first is a 'chicken and egg' dilemma. It will depend partly on which of the two is most likely to be booked up. A quick phone call will very soon establish the availability of both, although the end result may be a series of rapid fire calls (unless you can afford a party line!). You may have to make arrangements for someone who is available during office hours to make the enquiries, since that is the only time some people can be contacted.

Whether we use our own premises or a commercial venue, we need to check that the owners have been licensed by the Performing Rights society, and to ensure that a PRS returns form is available for the musician to complete with details of songs performed at the event.

The other main question at this stage concerns the cost of hire. It is important to check whether the figure quoted includes VAT, and whether any of the facilities you require will be charged separately. In our example, we discover that the use of the kitchen is extra.

Now that we have all the necessary information and have made a provisional booking, we are in a position to confirm in writing. Most public venues will require a booking form and/or contract to be completed and signed. Normally, this will be accompanied by a set of conditions for hire. Make sure that you have read these thoroughly, and if there are any queries that these have been addressed to the manager. I have discovered that most managers are happy to waive conditions provided they are happy that their facilities are not being used for any untoward or dangerous activity.

Hire of equipment

We have to hire lights for our musician and provide a large screen for his audio-visual equipment. We find the most economical hire firm through yellow pages (they agreed to give a discount of 10% since we are a church). We check with them when the equipment has to be collected and returned. It is worth knowing that it must be returned on the Sunday between 11am and 12 noon. We can arrange for someone to take it back, with several weeks notice, rather than expect someone to opt out of the family service at short notice! We can now confirm the booking in writing.

We have discovered that crockery is not available for use at the civic centre so we have arranged to borrow all that we need from a nearby church. This shows the importance of taking time to list all the equipment that will be needed and checking that it is available. Even something as basic as chairs may be missing – if we are expecting up to 100 people at an event, but the hall only has seating available for 40, we need to rectify the situation.

MAKING THE PREPARATIONS

Personnel

The number of people needed to help depends on the number of jobs to be done. The following list shows the range of functions:
- stewarding,
- shifting equipment,
- operating equipment,
- selling tickets (in advance and on the night),
- designing, producing and distributing publicity,
- arranging printing of tickets,
- bookstall,
- providing and preparing food/refreshments,
- compering the event,
- counselling,
- follow-up.

Each event will need a different complement of personnel. For our particular event we shall need: 2 stewards; 4 equipment shifters; 1 publicity/ticket distributor; 1 bookstall attendant; 1 compere; 10

counsellors (experience shows that on average 10% of an audience respond to high profile evangelistic appeals); 4 nurture group leaders; 2 cooks; 4 waiters/waitresses; 4 people to wash-up; 1 person to collect, return and operate lights/screen. This may seem quite a large number, but it is possible to make good use of resources by: doubling-up on jobs – for example, the ticket distributor could also look after the bookstall; people other than the young marrieds in the church would be used to cook and serve the food (leaving the young marrieds free to concentrate on their guests); some tasks like counselling and follow-up can be done by members of the group even though they have invited friends to the event and will be sitting with them. It is important to ensure that someone is responsible for each job, and that each section (eg food) is overseen by one person. In our case we have an organizing group of five people who each take responsibility for one of the following areas: food; counselling and follow-up; setting-up the venue/equipment; publicity; event programme.

In order to ensure that every aspect of organization is covered, list the jobs that need doing, subdividing them into various elements (see fig 8a). Against each element note the name of the person taking responsibility, and the date when the job must be completed. Use this information as a checklist so that the chief co-ordinator can check on progress. It is essential to be generous in allocating time for job completion.

When jobs have been allocated, ensure that each person responsible knows exactly what is expected of them. This can be done through issuing job descriptions. For example, the equipment shifters' brief would include:

- Arrive at civic centre no later than 3.30pm.
- Help musician transport equipment into the venue.
- Help transport lighting equipment into venue.
- Set out tables and chairs as directed by catering organizer.
- Help clear up hall after event – remove chairs and tables, sweep hall.
- Load music and lighting equipment into car.

This standard of organization will ensure that everyone knows what they should be doing. If it is done effectively the event will run

Job area	Task	Responsibility	Target for completion	Actual completion
PUBLICITY		John Marsh	23 Sept	
	Poster/handbill design	Viv Tarrant	14 June	
	Arrange printing	Roger Tyne	21 June	
	Co-ordinate handbill distribution	Gill Black	15 Sept	
	Contact press	Amanda Hynde	8 Sept	
	Poster distribution	Roger Tyne	11 Sept	
BOOKINGS		Ian Tidyman	14 March	
	Book musician/ speaker	Ian	1 Jan	
	Book venue	Ian	1 Jan	
	Hire PA/ lights	Paul Tidyman	1 June	

FIG. 8a

very smoothly and will give a good impression to those attending. After several such events, helpers will automatically know what their job entails, but it is still a good idea to keep a tight check on each aspect of the preparation.

Training

Counsellors and nurture group leaders/disciplers will need to be trained. If you do not already have a pool of trained people to fill these roles, you will have to make this a high priority before the event. It is vital to ensure adequate follow-up is available (see chapter 7). Counselling will be considered in depth in the following chapter.

Prayer

Even though we are concerned with the nitty-gritty of organizing, it is essential to keep prayer at the top of our agenda. Is the whole of the church aware of the event? Are members aware of specific prayer requests? Are there meetings when people can come together to pray for the event in particular? Do people know about these meetings and their importance? If the answer to any of these questions is 'no' you will need to act quickly in order to remedy the situation.

Publicity

We shall consider publicity in greater detail in chapter 10. In the meantime we need to consider some general points when preparing for an event. If the event is to be open to the general public then we should consider sending publicity to local papers, local radio, other churches, libraries, schools and colleges, in addition to the members of our church. As our particular example is lower key and limited to a specific clientele (friends of church members), publicity will be more personal. There will be posters around the church to remind members, and each will have a handbill to encourage them to remember the date and begin asking their friends. Closer to the event they will be given invitation cards to use. They will need to be reminded at meetings, but more importantly, individually. The personal touch is most effective. Some will need prompting, and perhaps help in thinking of who they could invite.

Tickets

Some events will need tickets – certainly our dinner and cabaret will, if only to know numbers for catering. Tickets will need to be printed and priced before being made available.

How much should you charge for an evangelistic event? This is a controversial question. Some would argue that we should never charge a person to hear the gospel. However, free events are often treated with suspicion. Paying for an event gives it value, and rouses expectations. In my experience, an event is more likely to attract people if it charges for entry, even if only a nominal sum. There is the question of covering costs, so in our example the cost of food and fees of a quality musician and speaker will be met out of ticket money.

If an event would have an entrance charge in a non-Christian environment, I would follow suit and price the ticket accordingly. Equally, I would not be averse to asking Christians to pay for their friends, or offering discounts to people we specifically want to reach. In my work in schools, if I am keen to attract young people to an evening event, then I will offer a generous discount. This is available to those who present a handbill (only available in their school) when they arrive at the ticket kiosk.

Counselling and follow-up

This is worth stressing again. All arrangements must be made well in advance of an event. Who will counsel, and who will follow-up? Have they been through the training? What material will they be using?

Event programme

This needs to be settled in advance and agreed by all the participants. The dinner and cabaret event will start at 7.30pm with dinner. After coffee has been served at about 8.20pm, the musician will play a 40-minute set and the speaker will be left with 20 minutes. The compere will introduce the evening and the musician, but the speaker has asked for the musician to hand straight over to him.

THE EVENT

Entry

Will the building be open when we wish to gain access, or do we have to make other arrangements? It is surprising how often this small but important point is overlooked. Organizers are advised to find out:

- How to gain access to the building.
- Arrangements for leaving the building at the end of the event.
- Where the lighting and heating switches are located.
- Where cleaning equipment is kept.
- The location of any other equipment to be used on the night.

Setting-up

All setting-up will need to be completed at least half an hour before the event is due to start. Be generous in the amount of time allowed for setting up technical equipment since there are often problems (mostly caused by simple faults such as the fuse or the bulb blowing, or a loose connection somewhere in the system). If there is more than one performing act in the programme, make sure that each has enough setting-up time, and that each is aware of the other's needs.

Briefing

Stewards and counsellors will probably need to meet for a briefing immediately before their task begins. It is advisable to spend some of that time in prayer for the event and specifically for their part in it. Indeed, it is no bad thing for a group of people to be praying throughout the event itself.

Counselling

This will occur at the end of the event. See chapter 9.

AFTER THE EVENT

Clearing up

Make sure that you have enough helpers to do the job thoroughly. Whatever the venue, always aim to leave it in a better condition than when you arrived. This in itself is a good witness.

Follow-up

It is vital that new Christians are contacted within the next 48 hours, so the follow-up co-ordinator will need to make arrangements as soon after the event as possible. If one-to-one discipling is the chosen method, then disciplers will need to be linked with converts and given all the counselling information. In our example we would ideally want to see new Christians being discipled by the friends who brought them along, provided they have been through the training for disciplers. This is because there is already a relationship and a trust on which to build. If nurture groups or enquirers' groups are the order of the day, these need to be arranged with equal speed.

Payments

Some participants will need to be paid on the night – remember to take a cheque-book! All outstanding payments should be made as soon after the event as possible.

Thank you letters

It is good policy to thank all those who helped towards the event, preferably in writing. All the main participants and team leaders should be thanked in this way. Include information about the outcome of the counselling to encourage them.

Review and assessment

Ensure that the main organizers meet to assess the organization and achievements of the event, and to take note of any lessons that can be learnt.

THE COST

As a guide to costs involved in an event we shall use our example. Our list of expenditure includes: fees for the speaker (£50) and musician (£100); hire of suite (£100), kitchen (£25), lighting (£30) and screen (£5); donation for loan of crockery (£10); production of tickets (£10) and publicity (£20); food (£500); counselling and follow-up material (£20); administrative costs (£10). This amounts to a total of £880.00, of which £750.00 will be covered by ticket sales (a hundred tickets costing £7.50 each) and the balance will be met from the church's evangelism fund.

We must be realistic in our budgeting – it is certainly not guaranteed that every event will be a sellout.

ORGANIZING ACTIVITIES

Most of the above applies to organizing evangelistic activities. The main difference is that church members are the main participants. The activities do not need a specialist or an artiste in order to work: the onus is all on the local Christians. This is especially so in door-to-door, street evangelism and coffee-bar work.

In this kind of work there will be greater emphasis on training and preparation. Every participant must be enabled to fulfil his or her role, and it is advisable to use specialist organizations for training, at least in the initial stages. There may be a member of the group who is able to carry out such training, but make sure that they know their subject, and that they are competent in leading a training session.

Once the activity has been planned – you know when and where it will take place, and you have all the necessary equipment – make sure that every participant has been informed, and that they will actually be there. It is no good making a general announcement in a church service and hoping that people will turn up. They will need to be approached individually and asked to give an assurance that they will be there – if necessary ask them to sign a list. An ad-hoc arrangement may work once, but not consistently. Check on each person before each day of an activity – it is hard work, but it will pay dividends.

ORGANIZING MISSIONS

It is very easy to get carried away organizing the high-profile, intensive period of a mission. Grandiose plans can lead to big events with disappointing audiences or disappointing results, or both. We are in danger of creating nothing more than a lot of noise and activity. Our aim should always be to bring people into the kingdom of God, and we must seek to do this as effectively and efficiently as possible.

For the sake of convenience, I shall use the term 'mission' as most people understand it – as a short period of intensive evangelistic events and activities. As I have pointed out elsewhere in this book, however, this period should be the focal point of a long-term strategy and process (see p115).

PLANNING A PROGRAMME

There are several factors that need to be considered when planning a programme for this big mission. These include:

1. The regular programme of evangelism

A mission should build on the evangelistic work that is already a part of the life of the church. It can be used as a focus for personal witnessing: Christians can invite the people to whom they have been talking about their faith. It can also be a focus for a series of evangelistic events or activities – maybe they have been building up to a high point. A mission will raise the profile of any evangelistic programme and it should be planned with this in mind. However, evangelistic activity should not end with a mission: once the profile has been raised it will create further interest which needs to be utilized.

2. Intensity

The kind of approach that has been agreed will determine this. The higher the profile required, the greater the intensity of activity. This will depend on the resources that are available. How much manpower is available? How much work can be undertaken by speakers and artistes bearing in mind that it is unwise to work more than two out of the three sessions (morning, afternoon, evening) in one day? How much time is left after preparation, setting-up and travelling time is taken into account? Has time been allowed for informal conversations with individuals? Are more events being organized than can be comfortably manned?

3. Length

The duration of a mission depends on the resources which are available, and also on the amount of effort needed from people to maintain a high standard of work. Do the opportunities warrant intensive activity? If the achievements of one week of mission are disappointing given the effort taken, then it is clear that a two-week mission would not be advisable.

4. Balance

What range of events should be used? This depends on who we are trying to reach. Are we aiming at the whole spectrum of people in a particular area? Or are we being specific – reaching young people or families or men only? Each event during the mission should have a specific objective. If we are trying to reach the whole spectrum, our events will reflect a wide range of interests, each event being targeted at one part of the spectrum – eg a rock concert for young people, a family activity on Saturday, Coffee mornings for mothers of young children, etc. If we are targeting a specific section of the population, the events should build on each other – eg a mission to men could begin with activities in factories and offices, unemployment centres, trade and labour clubs, pubs, snooker halls, etc. and build up to dinner and speaker evenings, or pizza and pint events.

5. Main participants

Organizers must liaise with the speakers and artistes who are taking part in the mission, to confirm the kind of activities which will be staged. For example, it is unwise to assume that any drama group will do street theatre – some do not have suitable material and others find their approach will not work in that situation. The artistes themselves may have ideas that had not been in the organizers' minds, but would be most appropriate.

Attendance at mission events will tend to grow as the week or weeks progress. The programme should reflect this, building toward a climax.

ORGANIZING THE EVENTS

Organizing mission events is very similar to organizing any evangelistic event. The main difference is the large number of activities and the intensity of the mission period. It is important to take precautions against overworking people and resources.

A timetable for the whole period of intensive mission activity will need to be prepared (see fig 8b overleaf for examples). Each of the guest speakers or artistes will need a personal timetable and, if they are visiting the area, a map. If possible, arrange for a church member to meet them and accompany them to the venue. If not, ensure that they have all the necessary information about where to go and who to contact at each venue.

Arrangements will have to be made for accommodation and meals. The pressure of working on a mission is intense, so participants need to be able to relax in their temporary home. Take care in choosing who to approach to ask to provide hospitality.

Missions are a focus of activity, so they should also be a focus of prayer. Timetables should be made available to those who have committed themselves to praying for the outreach.

LOCAL INVOLVEMENT

Local church members should be involved in mission activities wherever possible. This is very important. Don't limit them to setting up and clearing away. All the follow-up will be their responsibility, and so should all the counselling. Local Christians should be given exposure in the main events: some could tell the story of how they became Christians, for example, or talk about what God has been doing in their lives. At all activities, they should be open to the possibility of striking up conversations with those who come. Above all, they need to have built relationships with friends and neighbours to invite them along.

| SUMMARY |

- Organizing events:
  - □ Decide on style and aim of event.

□ Book the artiste(s)/speaker, venue and equipment hire.

□ Organize people to perform

MISSION TIMETABLE

Sunday

3pm	Team arrive at church. Taken by hosts to accommodation.
4pm	Team meeting – church.
5pm	Church tea.
6.30pm	Commissioning service.
8pm	Team leads youth fellowship meeting.

Monday

8.30am	Arrive at Plantins School to set up for assembly. Contact: Mr Hedger.
9am	Assembly.
9.15–12.15	Lessons (3 × 50 min 3rd year RE lessons).
12.15	School lunch.
12.45–1.10pm	Christian Union.
2pm	Team meeting – church.
8pm	House groups – evangelistic suppers – 32 Pitkin Way, 15 Hazel Drive, 'Rivendell', Chantry Avenue

Tuesday

9am	Team meeting – church.
10.30am	Evangelistic coffee mornings – church, 23 Hazel Drive, 42 Knox Road.
1pm	Digicloc – Christian Union open meeting.
8pm	Working Men's Club – Evangelistic presentation.
8.30pm	Fox & Hounds – 'Any Questions'.

Wednesday

9.15–12.15	Plantins School (2 × 4th yr/1 × 5th yr PSE lessons – 50 mins each).
12.15	School lunch.
1.20–2.10	Lesson (5th yr PSE).
7.30pm	Youth Coffee Bar – crypt.

Thursday

1pm	Team meeting/lunch – church.
2–3pm	Presentation – Walpole Junior School 4th year.
2.10–3.50pm	Plantins School – lessons (1 × 4th yr/1 × 5th yr).
6pm–7.30pm	Family Fun Event – church hall.
8pm	Businessmen's Dinner – Royal Arms Hotel.
	etc.

FIG. 8b

various tasks. Provide them with clear instructions.

□ Train counsellors, disciplers, nurture and enquirers' group leaders.

□Make arrangements for: prayer; publicity; tickets; counselling and follow-up; event programme.

□ Arrange for: entry into venue; setting up equipment and furniture, briefing stewards and counsellors; counselling.

□ After the event: clear up; follow up contacts; pay fees, expenses and bills; write thank you letters; review and assess event.

● Organizing activities: increased emphasis on training and preparation of church members to be involved in activity.

● Organizing missions (ie the intensive period of mission activity):

□ Planning the programme: take into account regular evangelistic activities, intensity and length of mission, balance of events to be used, opinions and skills of main participants.

□ Organize events as above.

□ Involve local people wherever possible.

| ACTION SHEET 8 |

EXERCISE 1

30 MINUTES – Working in pairs, plan an evangelistic event specified by the group leader. The following are examples that could be used:

□ A coffee bar event for teenagers, to include drama and speaker.

□ A family fun-day, with Christian ventriloquist.

□ A lunch-time event for businessmen.

□ Any event that would be suitable for your situation.

Each pair should establish the aim of the event, and then make detailed plans with a timescale, and suggestions of who should be responsible for each task. (See also figure 8a.)

EXAMPLE Coffee Bar. Aim: to show unchurched young people in the area that the Christian faith is relevant to them. Objective: to hold an informal coffee bar event at which a speaker with appeal to young people will speak. Method: personal visit and invitation. Youth group to invite their friends. Others to be

PRACTICALITIES

visited and invited include: past members of church youth organizations and Sunday School, contacts made through annual holiday club, brothers and sisters of children attending church organizations. Use a table like this.

Task	Person responsible	Deadline	Completed
Book hall	Jean Gray	12 March	
Book speaker	Roger Hendricks	20 March	

20 MINUTES – Form pairs into foursomes to examine and comment on each others plans. Ensure that all criticism is constructive.

A LINK IN THE CHAIN

COUNSELLING AT EVENTS

Events are an unnatural setting for evangelism. Jesus did not organize 'Gospel Outreach Events'. He simply talked to the people he met. He did not put on events to attract crowds: they were attracted to him naturally. He also went to places where the crowds already were, such as the Temple.

Ideally, people should become Christians through the witness of the words and deeds of believers, and sometimes the power of God demonstrated in signs and wonders. Even though the witness of the church is improving there is so much ground still to make up that we need events to supplement our personal evangelism. Events can create an opportunity to proclaim the message of the gospel, and they must be used as effectively as possible. We must try to ensure that everyone who responds to Christ's challenge to 'follow me' is helped. This is the role of the 'event counsellor'.

THE EVENT COUNSELLOR

Ultimately, the responsibility for bringing anyone to that point of commitment lies with the Holy Spirit. New birth is a supernatural process that happens in the natural realm with the permission of the individual. An event counsellor helps people to choose for themselves. Since the onus is on the Holy Spirit to convince and convict, and on the individual to decide, our task is to ensure that people understand what they are doing and that they are given all the necessary help. This is the task of the event counsellor. It must not be confused with 'counselling' in the generally accepted sense of the word, which is concerned with helping people to gain an insight into problems of various kinds. The event counsellor will not be in a position to offer that kind of help.

HOW NOT TO DO IT

All the following can create problems in event evangelism, and should be strongly avoided:

1. **Emotional manipulation** Writing as someone who regularly speaks at evangelistic events, I know just how responsible the task is. It is very easy, knowingly or unknowingly, to manipulate people to follow a course of action or respond in a particular way. Emotional pressure will produce a response at an emotional level. This is particularly true of a concert, because music taps the emotions. It is not surprising that people get very excited at rock concerts, carried along by the beat and uplifted by soaring guitar solos. But becoming a Christian should not be based on an emotional decision alone. It is not only feelings, but also fact and faith that form the basis of Christian belief.

I am not saying that emotions are not involved – who can blame someone for the elation they feel when they realize they are totally forgiven for all the wrong in their life? Nor am I saying that the Holy Spirit does not use the emotions to draw a person to Christ. The warning that I am giving is to be aware of the dangers of emotionalism, and to do our utmost to defuse any emotions that are not moved by God. There is nothing worse than someone who 'gives their life to God' in the heat of the moment only to find that they regret what they have done once their emotions have subsided. God wants our whole lives, not just our emotions. Likewise, he does not want our lives without our emotions!

2. **Lack of organization** I have attended evangelistic events where the organizers have been caught off-balance by the response to the gospel. The organization of the counselling has been a shambles, so that by the time enough people have been found to talk with enquirers, several have left and those who remain are bewildered. In

addition, the impromptu counsellors often have no idea of what is expected of them.

My experience shows that on average ten per cent of an audience in an evangelistic event will respond to the challenge. Several factors will affect whether the end result is higher or lower: the style of the evangelist; the style of the event; whether it is a single event or part of a series (there will be a higher response if it is towards the end of a series); the way in which an appeal to respond is issued; and most importantly, the degree to which the Holy Spirit is convincing and convicting people of their need to respond.

3. Lack of training Some organizers appear to believe that any Christian can counsel adequately at events. This is patently not the case. Most Christians find it difficult to explain succinctly how to become a Christian. In the excitement of the situation, many Christians think that the reason for someone being there is that they want to make a commitment to Christ, so without asking they plough on. This is at best unfortunate. For all they know, they may be talking with someone who has lost his way to the toilets. Event counsellors need training. I have found that most ordinary Christians are quite capable of counselling after they have been trained. A two-hour session is adequate to communicate all the necessary information and procedures. Extra time can be used for practice.

It is also important for counsellors at any event to be briefed about the routine – literature, counselling forms, follow-up arrangements, etc.

4. The numbers game Beware of falling into the trap of counting everyone who is counselled as making a Christian commitment. Normally only a proportion will have made a commitment at that stage. Moreover, only time will show whether that step of faith is genuine and lasting.

It was a mixture of these problems that eventually forced me to reconsider how counselling should be organized at the events I arranged. I selected local Christians who I felt could help with counselling. Those who agreed were given a specially written handbook to read, and were then given two hours of training. As a result we have thirty people who can be called on to counsel at our events with enough preparation to do the job well. The rest of this chapter outlines the procedures that we follow, and can be adapted to your situation with ease. Even if you choose not to follow them in detail, they are based on several sound principles that underlie all effective event counselling.

EVENT COUNSELLING GUIDELINES[1]

BEFORE THE EVENT

Counsellors need to come to the event fully prepared. They should have reviewed the instructions they were given at their training session, and should be familiar with any literature to be used in counselling. They should bring:

- A Bible (pocket-sized modern translation, to show specific verses or passages if applicable).
- A pen (to complete the counselling form – it will need to be a biro or pencil if the form is NCR duplicate).
- A clean handkerchief (in case things become emotional).

They should arrive at the event promptly for a pre-event briefing by the co-ordinator of counselling. This will include:

- Instructions specific to that event.
- The evangelist explaining the gist of his message and the planned format for the appeal.
- The opportunity to familiarize themselves with the counselling area, and how to reach it from the main venue. (The closer it is, the better.)
- Collecting a counsellor's badge which acts as a means of identification. These should have the counsellor's name on them. Avoid putting 'Counsellor' on them. There is no need to wear the badge through the event – it may be distracting or off-putting to non-Christians. Only put it on when it is necessary to identify yourself as a counsellor.
- The opportunity to pray for each other and for the event.

Such briefings will need 20–30 minutes.

THE APPEAL

The subject of evangelistic appeals warrants a whole book[2]. They are controversial, and certain sections of the church strongly object to their use. Nevertheless appeals are used extensively in event evangelism, and are extremely useful in encouraging individuals to respond to Christ's claim on their life.

Appeals vary from speaker to speaker and situation to situation. Some appeal to the audience to commit their life to following Christ; some to come 'closer to Christ'; others to express an interest in discovering more about Christianity. The form of appeal can cause problems: if the evangelist appeals for people to commit their lives to Christ, how do those who are interested, but not yet ready to commit themselves, respond?

This is clearly an area that the organizers must discuss with the evangelist beforehand. It goes far beyond the practical aspects of organization. The aim is to see genuine conversions – changes of heart and mind, which should not be treated lightly. The evangelist must understand clearly whether their approach will enable genuine conversions to occur, or hinder it. The organizers must satisfy themselves that the evangelist they wish to use has taken these considerations into account.

To go into these matters in greater depth is beyond the scope of this book, so we shall leave this to the reader to pursue elsewhere and move on to deal with the practical aspect of coping with the results of an appeal.

Once an appeal has been made, people can be asked to show a response in various ways – eg: stand up; raise a hand in the air; come to the front; go to the counselling area; come and chat afterwards. I have even come across 'hold your hymn book in a peculiar way' as one method!

After the appeal and the response, the next vital stage is linking those who have responded with counsellors. Between them, organizer and evangelist must do their utmost to ensure a smooth link-up. In a large event there are two methods that seem most appropriate. In the first, people respond by coming to the front. The evangelist's 'friends' (ie the counsellors) also come out and introduce themselves to individuals as directed by the evangelist. Together they go to the counselling area for a conversation. The second method is similar, except that those who respond are directed to the counselling area where the co-ordinator links them with counsellors.

Even when the method of linking-up has been agreed by the evangelist and co-ordinators, it may be changed at the discretion of the evangelist if he or she feels another method is more appropriate. Counsellors will therefore need to listen carefully to the evangelist's instructions and must follow them without hesitation. Counsellors should have put on their badges by this stage.

There are two golden rules for linking up. The first is that only in exceptional circumstances should a counsellor be talking to more than one person. One-to-one is best, since the response should be individual rather than a case of following the crowd. The second rule is that counselling of the opposite sex should be avoided. Occasionally difficult situations arise when unhelpful emotions are sparked off. This may sound silly, but it does happen.

The counselling co-ordinator will need to be on the look out for problems in linking up and must be prepared to think on his feet and provide quick and effective solutions.

BUILDING BRIDGES

Although counselling will take place over a short period of time, it is important for the counsellor to establish a friendly relationship out of which they can help the other person. Getting on first-name terms straightaway will help, as will a few general questions to find out more about them. (During the rest of this chapter I shall use the term counsellee for the person being counselled. I dislike the term since it depersonalizes the description, but there is no other that can be used.)

Once settled into a quiet corner, the counsellor will need to establish what position the counsellee is in. A simple question such as 'Why have you come to chat?' is both non-threatening and allows them to use their own words. If no reply is forthcoming suggest a few alternatives from which they can choose (eg 'Is it because you want to become a Christian, or do you just want to find out more, or don't you really know why. . ?'). Once they have replied, the counsellor is in a much better position to continue.

There are two possible reasons why they may not give a sensible answer. The first is that they may be too emotional. In this case, let them calm down and then proceed. If they remain too emotional make arrangements with the co-ordinator for someone to see them within the next day or two when they will have recovered. The second possibility is that they are messing around. This occurs most often at youth events. If it is obvious that they are not serious, the counsellor should concentrate on developing a friendly relationship with them by chatting generally.

If the counsellee has given a sensible reply they can be helped further. We shall deal with each reply in turn.

'I want to become a Christian'
Your conversation should work through the following stages:

1. Ask the question 'Why?' This will help the counsellor to understand exactly where the person is coming from, and will give them an idea whether the counsellee understands what becoming a Christian involves.

2. Check that they understand what becoming a Christian involves. Jesus taught us to count the cost, and a person considering following him must have an idea of what they are letting themselves in for:

□ A CHANGE OF HEART – conversion involves repentance: turning away from disobedience to God. This means a change in attitude and behaviour. The Holy Spirit gives the power to do this.

□ A CHANGE OF BOSS – conversion involves submitting to the Lordship of Christ. Instead of being in charge of my own life I put God in control.

□ A CHANGE OF LOYALTIES – conversion involves a life-long commitment to following Jesus. This should affect every area of my life.

□ A CHANGE OF LIFESTYLE – conversion involves getting to know God – talking with him and finding out more about him. Prayer, Bible reading, meeting with other Christians, and telling others about him should become a regular part of our lives.

For most people these are major changes. They need to realize that they will discover many new and exciting things after becoming a Christian. Much of this will be done through a nurture group or in one-to-one discipling, so follow-up arrangements should be explained at this point, so they know they can have help.

3. **Check that they know how to become a Christian**. There are various ways of explaining this, but the three basic elements are:

☐ REPENTANCE – ie turning away from sin (doing the things God does not want us to do or not doing the things he does want), and turning towards God.

☐ FAITH – accepting and believing that Jesus is God, and that when he died on the cross he took all our sin on himself. As a result, God can now forgive our sins, and we can have a relationship with him, through Jesus Christ.

☐ OBEDIENCE – this is for life. At the start of the Christian life it should involve two specific aspects: 'Be baptised' (Acts 2:38) and 'Be filled with the Spirit' (Ephesians 5:18).

The counsellor will need to explain these points, making sure they are understood. They should avoid jargon words such as 'redemption', and be sure to explain those, such as 'sin', that are used.

4. **Check that they are sure they want to become a Christian**. The question should be phrased so that the counsellee is given an option. For example, 'Do you want to become a Christian now, or would you like to wait and think about it, or would you rather leave it?'

5. **Making a commitment**. When the counsellee is ready to make a commitment, whether at the event or at a later date, they will need to pray. The commitment is between the individual and God. They should be encouraged to pray out loud, whether they do so in their own words, reading from a book, or repeating the counsellor's prayer sentence by sentence. The prayer should be simple and should include the following elements:

'I am sorry for not obeying you.'

'Please forgive me, and help me to turn from doing wrong.'

'Thank you Lord Jesus for dying for me on the cross so that I can have the best kind of life.'

'I want to follow you for the rest of my life – please help me to do this.'

'Come into my life through your Holy Spirit. Thank you.'

The counsellor should then pray for the new Christian, that God would help them in the early stages of their new life. They can lay on hands and ask for God to fill them with his Holy Spirit.

'I am interested and want to know more'

The counsellor should explain what it means to be a Christian and how to become one as above. The counsellee may then want to make a commitment. If they are not ready, the option of an enquirers' group may be offered.

'I became a Christian in the event'

The counsellor needs to make sure that the new Christian understands what they have done, that they realize what it means to be a Christian, and that they can be helped through the follow-up. Generally the new Christian will need encouragement and prayer.

It may turn out that the counsellee is not ready to make a commitment and needs time to think it over. They will need to be reassured that God does not think any the less of them. Indeed, he prefers his followers to count the cost. An enquirers' group will probably be the best form of follow-up in this instance.

'I have a problem'

Very few people would actually say this, but their reply may amount to the same thing. The counsellor needs to discover exactly what the problem is. If they are out of their depth they should refer back to the counselling co-ordinator immediately so that someone can be found who is able to help. At our events I try to ensure that amongst our counsellors there is someone trained in pastoral counselling, someone experienced in dealing with demonic oppression, and someone who has expertise in helping victims of rape or child abuse. This sounds very high-powered, and is only really necessary at very large events. However it is worthwhile compiling a list of local people who can help in these areas. If they cannot attend the event they can be contacted afterwards.

If the counsellor can help with the problem, either with advice or practically, they must still refer it back to the counselling co-ordinator. This is to avoid treading on the toes of any church leaders who are already involved in the situation. At the very least they should pray with the counsellee.

'I don't know'

The counsellor should try to discover the reason behind any response to an appeal. Sometimes people genuinely do not know why they respond. Use of questions such as 'Did you enjoy the event? Why/why not?' can be a profitable line of approach.

GENERAL GUIDELINES

The following guidelines, known as the 'Four Be's', should be applied in all situations:

1. **Be understandable**. Avoid using religous jargon and clichés. Redemption, justification and sanctification are not words in common use, and will leave most people baffled. Even words like sin may not be understood. The counsellor should make sure they are being understood by asking the counsellee to explain what they have heard and understood. It can be very revealing! Avoid merely asking, 'Do you understand?' or the counsellee will respond, 'Yes' and you will be none the wiser!

2. **Be fair**. The counsellee should never be pushed into a corner so that they make a commitment because they feel they do not have any other choice. One of God's greatest gifts is free will. We should respect this by always offering alternatives when posing a question. That way, there is always a way out. There is great danger in asking a question which demands a yes or no response since the person answering is tempted to give the answer that will please the questioner.

3. **Be honest**. The Christian life should not be glamorized. It is a great life, but it is not always easy. The counsellor should underline the seriousness of making a Christian commitment. He should also avoid using platitudes at all cost.

4. **Be certain**. It is better for a person to wait and think things through than to be pushed into becoming a Christian reluctantly.

This can often leave a sour after-taste, and very unhealthy resentment.

THE COUNSELLING FORM

Make a record every time someone is counselled. This will ensure that no-one is forgotten in the follow-up, and that if there is any query, the co-ordinator can check back to discover the details of the counselling conversation.

A form is probably the best method of keeping a record. It can be printed or photocopied onto paper or card. I use triplicate forms so that I can keep a copy, and the others can be used by those responsible for follow-up.

Our example (see fig 9) has several aspects that need to be highlighted. It is important to make sure that there is plenty of information on:

☐ the counsellee,
☐ the conversation,
☐ appropriate methods for continuing contact.

It is vital to ensure that follow-up is made as easy as possible. The co-ordinator needs to know the exact situation, any circumstances that are relevant, and the best means of contacting the counsellee.

I normally advise our counsellors to complete the basic information as they are counselling. They will need to explain what they are doing and why, so that the counsellee is at ease. Details about the conversation should be completed immediately afterwards. Needless to say, the form is confidential and as few people as possible should see it, particularly if it contains sensitive information.

LITERATURE IN COUNSELLING

There are many pamphlets designed to help interested people. They are particularly useful for giving to counsellees to read in their own time. Match the material with the person, taking into account their age, ability range, and their particular circumstances. It is no good giving a very academic booklet to someone who can barely read! Don't overload enquirers with reading material. Be selective. Organizers should choose a basic selection of pamphlets, and encourage counsellors to familiarize themselves with the range.

ST OGG'S CHURCH:
EVENT COUNSELLING FORM

Counsellor's name _____

Event _____ Date _____

DETAILS

Name _____ Age (approx if 21+) ____

Address _____

_____

Job (or school/college name) _____

Church connection _____
(ie which church & how connected)

Reason for attending _____
(eg who brought them)

CONVERSATION

Tick as appropriate

☐ Wants to know more about becoming a Christian. . . .

☐ Wants to become a Christian. . . .

☐ Wants greater commitment. . . .

☐ Has a problem

☐ Other

CONVERSATION DETAILS

Literature taken _____

Best form of contact (circle) Phone Letter Visit Through contact –
Name _____

FOLLOW-UP
Arrangements:

Booklets fall into the following categories:
- ☐ How to become a Christian.
- ☐ How to live as a Christian (vital for those who have made a commitment).
- ☐ Bible reading notes (to encourage regular Bible reading).
- ☐ A Gospel (for those who want to find out more about Jesus).

(See Resources List for recommended material).

LINKING INTO THE FOLLOW-UP

Making the link between this counselling and the follow-up is the responsibility of those co-ordinating these areas. It may or may not be the same person. Counselling and follow-up co-ordinators must clarify the procedure for initiating follow-up. They must decide in advance who makes the arrangements in each individual case.

Ideally there should be continuity between the counselling and the follow-up. This may mean that the counsellor is involved in follow-up, or even a Christian friend of the new believer. In either case they must have been trained in follow-up techniques. If this is not possible, for example because follow-up is in a nurture group, and the leader has been chosen, then it is helpful for the leader to be in the counselling room so that members for the group can be introduced and contact made. Indeed, it is an advantage if arrangements for the first follow-up session can be made there and then, especially if a group is involved. It will be quicker to find a mutually convenient time and date.

Where the counsellor cannot be involved in follow-up, he or she may still be able to maintain contact with the new Christian or enquirer provided they do not cut across the discipler or nurture group leader.

AFTER THE COUNSELLING

As soon as the counselling is over, the counselling form should be returned to the co-ordinator, who can check that they have enough information. The badge can also be returned.

In the following days and weeks, the counsellor should continue to pray for the person with whom they talked, and, if agreed with the co-ordinator, can write to them or chat over the phone to give them encouragement.

CRUCIAL

Event counselling is a crucial link in a chain of events that leads to genuine Christian commitment. In my experience, it is often the point at which evangelistic events break down. This is why I have gone into so much detail in this chapter.

Above all else, our desire in evangelistic events is to see individuals come into a meaningful and personal relationship with the living Lord Jesus Christ, and to grow into a mature faith as a true disciple. Our concern is that all should have the opportunity to come to this decision in a reasoned, non-pressurized way. Following Christ is too serious to be treated lightly. In all we do we must keep in balance our desire and our concern. This balance should be the key-note in our counselling: we want to encourage people to commit their lives to the Lord, but never to put them under any psychological or emotional pressure. God may well bring them under conviction in a way that involves the emotions, but that is the role of the Holy Spirit under the sovereign will of God.

| NOTES |

1. Adapted from *Event Counselling Handbook*, Malcolm Egner, Welwyn Hatfield Youth For Christ, 1986.

2. There are several books on the subject of appeals, among the best is *The Christian Persuader*, Leighton Ford (Harper and Row, 1976).

| SUMMARY |

• Role of event counsellor: to help people to make genuine decision to commit their lives to Christ.

• Problems in event evangelism include: emotional appeals and manipulation; lack of organization of event counselling; lack of training of counsellors; obsession with size of response.

- Guidelines for counselling:
  □ Counsellors should arrive early and fully prepared.
  □ They should be briefed about evangelist's message and type of appeal.
  □ Link-up between enquirers and counsellors needs to be planned in advance and with care.
  □ Counsellor needs to establish friendly relationship quickly
  □ Counsellor needs to discover the counsellee's reasons for responding, and to be able to deal with all the following:

'I want to become a Christian.'
'I am interested and want to know more.'
'I became a Christian in the event.'
'I need help with a problem.'
'I don't know why I responded.'
  □ Counsellors should be understandable; fair; honest; and certain.
  □ Counselling forms are vital for recording information.
  □ Use literature in counselling with discernment.

- Arrangements for linking into the follow-up should be planned in advance and with care.

| ACTION SHEET 9 |

EXERCISE 1
30 MINUTES – Individually, work out how you would explain 'How to become a Christian'. After 10–15 minutes preparation, find a partner, and practise your explanation. The explanation should be no longer than five minutes. Your partner will comment on the good and bad aspects of your presentation. Was it easy to understand? Did it make sense? Was it theologically sound? etc. Swap roles.

EXERCISE 2
10 MINUTES – Each pair will role-play an event counselling situation. The person who is to be 'counselled' will be given a card containing the role they are to play. It could be one of the following:
  □ You don't really know why you responded to the evangelistic challenge. You are a little bit emotional and did not want to be left out when your friends responded.

□ You are a young teenager who wants to become a Christian, but whose parents will be very hostile to the idea – if they ever find out you will not be allowed to continue.

□ You have been fiddling the books at work, and have been challenged by the event. You are loth to actually admit what you have been doing.

□ You are interested in becoming a Christian, but have problems with the question of suffering. This is the result of seeing a close relative suffering and eventually dying of cancer.

Also include some cards that are more straightforward, eg You want to become a Christian.

5 MINUTES – In pairs discuss how the conversation developed.

10 MINUTES – Ask each pair to share with the whole group any problems that arose, and any lessons to be learnt.

One variation on this is to have a pair act out their roles in front of the whole group and then ask for comments. This can be very daunting so the group leader should ensure that positive encouragement is the key to group discussion.

PREPARE THE WAY
PUBLICITY AND PRAYER

The plans have been made, resources obtained and people mobilized. You are almost ready to go, but there is one final element to the organization of evangelistic events and missions – publicity.

Let us not labour under a false impression, however. Publicity does not bring the people in. It is not the solution to poor attendance. People are not usually attracted to an activity through publicity alone, at least in the local situation. Far more important is personal invitation and the credibility of Christian friends – the prayer, witness and friendship which have been stressed throughout this book.

If that is the case, why is publicity so important?

PROJECTING THE RIGHT IMAGE

Good publicity gives an event credibility. If a poster is well designed and produced, it tells the public something about the quality of the event it is advertising. People are more likely to come to an event if they think it will be worth attending, so the publicity must convey the right impression. Design and production quality are equally important. Unfortunately, much of the church's publicity is so old-fashioned that it would not be out of place in the 1950's or 60's! We need to be up-to-date and imaginative in our publicity.

PUBLICITY CO-ORDINATOR

From the outset, a publicity co-ordinator is vital. He or she will need to plan a publicity campaign, and ensure that all efforts work towards that campaign. What image do we want to project? How much publicity do we need and of which kind? Who will design the publicity ... print it ... distribute it? Help is given with all these aspects in this chapter.

One of the keys to effective advertising is simply the number of times people see the name of a product. If I am faced by an array of similar products when I go shopping, I will tend to buy the brand with which I am most familiar. The more often I have seen a name, the more likely I will be to consider it a good product, even though I have no real evidence that this is the case. We need to learn from this, and to note how important a name and logo will be in projecting the right image.

The name should communicate something about the event and yet avoid being corny or predictable. I am dismayed by the lack of imagination and creativity amongst organizers of Christian events. The name is important, and time should be spent deciding on it. Titles such as 'Sonblest' or 'Sonshine' should be banished immediately. By all means use a little intrigue, but surely our ingenuity is greater than this. Nor is it necessary always to include some kind of reference to the Godhead in our titles. A series of events organized for young people in my locality was called 'The Crunch'. This was an excellent title. It had immediate impact, was memorable, and managed to give the impression that there would be a hard-hitting evangelistic message without being at all off-putting. It was a title with no spiritual connotations whatsoever.

It is not easy to think of titles for missions – but they really do need to catch the imagination. Brainstorming sessions, in which a group of people meet together for a short time and throw out ideas can often produce good names. No-one is allowed to make any comment on the ideas until the time is up. Sometimes a name which might have been thrown out immediately proves to be ideal, or it leads on to another idea. Imaginations can run riot with surprising results, and if the final choice of names is a little daring, so much the better.

The logo is a design which is used to identify the event on all publicity. It may include the name. Again, it needs to be imaginative. Sometimes the idea will come from a church member, sometimes a graphic designer will be able to make suggestions.

The name and the logo provide an identity for the mission or event. A good name and a good logo will go a long way towards projecting the right image.

EVERYWHERE YOU GO

Posters and handbills are among the best ways for getting the name around. Posters can be put up in house windows, outside the venue, in shop windows, in libraries, community centres, colleges and schools. If this is done effectively, people will be confronted by the publicity almost everywhere they turn. Obviously, permission will need to be obtained in most of these places, but the majority of people who are asked will be obliging.

Handbills can be put through letter boxes, or left on windscreens in car parks. Most of them will probably be thrown straight into a rubbish bin, but at least people will have seen the main details. Handbills can also be left in libraries, clinics, waiting rooms, etc. Effective distribution needs to be carefully thought out. By far the most effective, however, is for Christians to personally invite their friends and acquaintances and use the handbill to give them details. If the handbill is attractively designed and produced it will give credibility to the event.

SOME PRACTICAL POINTERS

Design needs to be carefully planned too. Professional graphic designers can be used, but it is quite possible for the artistic amateur to produce good artwork. Keep in mind the following guidelines:

1. Posters need to catch the eye: simple designs are often the most effective. A well-designed poster is not cluttered; it uses space well.

2. Keep details to a minimum: event name, contributors, time, date, venue and prices are the bare essentials. They should stand out clearly.

3. Emphasize the most important points by putting them in a larger size, or using rules to underline them. Don't overcomplicate information by using too many different sizes or styles of lettering. Stick to two or three.

4. Experiment with different word spacing. Word spacing should never be haphazard (unless that is the point of the design). Try centring it, or lining up to one side. Figure 10 shows good and bad examples.

5. It is also important to give some indication of the Christian nature of the event. 'Youth for Christ present' or 'St Oggs Church present' will help towards that. When an evangelist will be speaking, I have often used something like 'Telling it like it is – a straightforward presentation of the Christian message'. This leaves the audience in no doubt as to what they are letting themselves in for.

Unless you have calligraphy skills or outstanding handwriting, dry transfer lettering ('Letraset' or similar) will look best – and it should always be used for large-scale events. Line drawings reproduce better than those with shading (half-tones). If shading is needed, dry transfer shading such as 'Letratone' can be used. However, it needs practice to get a good result.

The best size for handbills is A5, but posters can be used in a variety of sizes. A4 or at most A3 is suitable for noticeboards where space is limited. A2 may be used outside venues, etc. Before making the final decision, think through where they will be used.

Quantities also need to be planned in advance. How many posters are you likely to display? For handbills, how many houses will you be delivering to? How many will be used by individuals to invite others?

Posters and handbills can be reproduced by off-set litho or photocopying. For small quantities it is worthwhile photocopying, especially if your church has access to a good copier. Anything over 100 should always be printed.

If a photograph is used, this is best reproduced through printing. A plate will need to be made of the photograph: if you supply a good quality black and white print, the printer will screen it to the

St Oggs Church
present
The Joe Soap Band
in concert
The Memorial Hall,
Ridgely Road, Old Town
7.30 24th October
Tickets £2
Details OT 2143

St Oggs Church
present
THE
JOE SOAP
BAND
IN CONCERT
7.30pm Friday 24 October
The Memorial Hall,
Ridgely Road, Old Town
Tickets £2
Details: Tel. Old Town 2134

FIG. 10

size and shape you specify. A photocopier that copes with half-tones could be used, but this is generally only available commercially. Ordinary photocopiers rarely reproduce photographs well.

Your local printer will be able to advise you on what is best when you are producing a large volume of publicity for important events. He will also advise you how to present any artwork you are producing yourselves. It is wise to obtain several quotations before employing a printer, and ask to see examples of their work.

IN THE MEDIA

Local newspapers and radio provide further opportunities to get the message across.

Newspapers can be used in a variety of ways:

1. They may print articles about events and activities. One way of arousing the editor's interest is to send a press release. This is a summary of an item the newspaper may want to feature. It should contain all the main details of the activity, typed with double line

spacing. Any information which gives an unusual angle should also be included, as reporters are always on the lookout for a good story. Press releases should be distributed at least a week before the next edition is due out.

It is an advantage to build a good relationship with an editor or reporter – a personal phone call to a friendly reporter is usually more effective than contacting the paper's newsdesk. Articles in advance of the event will provide good publicity and reports afterwards, especially with photographs, are no bad thing.

2. The main disadvantage of having an article printed is that you cannot guarantee what will actually be written. Even the most carefully written press release can be turned upside-down and inside-out. It's a risk that has to be recognized. An advert costs money, but it does mean that you can put in whatever you want – although it may be hard to ensure it is put somewhere that will stand out. Ads can be taken with or without artwork provided. The latter would mean leaving the choice of design and typeface entirely in the hands of the newspaper. Even if artwork is provided, the newspaper may substitute its own typeface. I have discovered that supplying the logo with concise instructions for the size of lettering for typesetting suffices in most situations. I strongly advise discussing details with the advertising department of the paper.

3. An inexpensive way of using the paper to advertise is through the 'What's on' column. This is often free, but has the drawback that your event is more likely to be lost among a sea of jumble sales, dance classes and other local events.

Radio. Like newspapers, local radio can be used to broadcast reports about events, especially if they are newsworthy. Town-wide missions are more likely to attract coverage than individual church outreaches. Local radio often has a 'What's on' slot where local events are advertised. Contact the station office and ask how they can advertise events. Ask who deals with news items, and speak to that person by name. Be warned – it is easy to get evangelistic events publicized on religious programmes, but it takes much greater effort to get a mention when more of the general public are listening. It is an effort worth making.

Radio need not be the limit. Local TV, especially community cable stations, may also provide opportunities to publicize your activities. An effective publicity co-ordinator needs to be persistent and adventurous!

MAKING AN IMPACT

We have by no means exhausted the methods of publicizing activities. Here are some further suggestions for ways of making an impact:

- street theatre,
- banners stretched over the high street or across a building,
- carnival float,
- car touring the streets with a loudspeaker,
- people (maybe in costume) handing out leaflets,
- exhibition/display in local library,
- crazy stunts in shopping precincts,
- hot-air balloons.

These may seem outrageous, but they will certainly grab people's attention. Make use of personal contacts, too. They may well produce the necessary equipment at a fraction of commercial rates.

The larger an event, the more publicity is needed. Interest can be increased by a 'teaser' campaign. This involves publicity that attracts attention without giving details in a build-up to the main advertising. For example, a series of 'The Crunch' could be preceded by posters appearing around the town with the words 'And when it comes to the Crunch. . .', but no other details. As the events draw nearer, posters with the relevant information would appear. The common factor would be the event's logo.

FULL CIRCLE

Another method of preparing the way and drawing attention to activities is the praise march. This has been brought back into vogue during the late '80's by singer-songwriter Graham Kendrick. His 'Make Way' material[1] has been used throughout the nation in villages, towns and cities, to raise the profile of Christianity and its message. The march includes songs and shouts proclaiming the greatness of God and the Lordship of Christ. It is taking the message out on to the streets.

The praise march has a double function. Firstly, it spreads the message to others, and secondly, it uses praise as a means of claiming territory for God. By praising God in places where he may not often be thought about, a victory for God is claimed in the spiritual battle for influence in people's lives.

It may seem strange to relate the task of sharing God's love with people in terms of warfare but that is exactly what it is. Paul writes that '. . . our struggle is not against flesh and blood, but against the rulers, against the authorities, against the powers of this dark world and against the spiritual forces of evil in the heavenly realms. Therefore put on the full armour of God. . .' (Ephesians 6:12–13). We must not underestimate the spiritual struggle, but should prepare ourselves by taking up the weapons of faith, hope and love. We are not fighting against the people that we are trying to reach, but against spiritual forces. Our fight must take the form of loving these people as Christ loves them.

At the beginning of this book I put forward the need for prayer to see the tide turn in this country. I return to this theme because it is so vital, and Paul refers to it in the context of spiritual warfare (Ephesians 6:18). As Christians we are concerned with raising the profile of our Lord – lifting the name of Jesus so that all can see, in the hope that all will acknowledge him as Lord and Saviour. Satan will do his utmost to prevent this. He will blind people to their need, and encourage apathy. Prayer is essential to combat these tactics. Such prayer must be God-centred, with praise as a major element.

Thus praise marches are only a part of this, albeit a very important part. Prayer walks around the locality interceding for the people can also be used. Meeting together for prayer through the night, or the day, or both, and fasting and praying, are mighty weapons too. We may not understand the spiritual dynamics of prayer, but there is little doubt that God wants us to do it. 'Pray continually' is our instruction (1 Thessalonians 5:17), and Jesus is our example – on one occasion he prayed for forty days.

Prayer can transform our evangelistic endeavours. Prayer touches the spiritual, and it is in the spiritual realm that people respond to God. By prayer we can *prepare the way*!

| NOTES |

1. *Make Way, Shine Jesus Shine (Make Way 2), Make Way for Christmas (The Gift)* and *Make Way for the Cross* are available on record and cassette, and in book form.

Some of the books include the background to and instructions for organizing praise marches. (Kingsway Publications)

| SUMMARY |

• The most effective publicity is personal invitation and recommendation.

• Publicity should be used to project the right image. Its main purpose is to give an event credibility.

• One of the keys to effective publicity is the number of times people see the name. Therefore name and logo are important.

• Handbills and posters should be displayed wherever possible. Handing out leaflets needs to be carefully planned in order to be most effective.

• Make your material as effective as possible by using the most appropriate design and production techniques.

• Activities can be publicized through the media:

   □ Newspapers – send press releases for articles, use advertising space, use free 'What's on' guides

   □ Radio – news items, 'What's on' items.

   □ Regional and cable television.

• Be creative in making a visual impact on the community.

• Use prayer and praise marches to prepare the way.

| ACTION SHEET 10 |

EXERCISE 1

10 MINUTES EACH – In groups of four or five, 'brainstorm' on any or all of the following:

□ the name for a planned evangelistic event or series of events,

□ the name for a mission (planned or hypothetical),

□ places where posters could be displayed or handbills used.

EXERCISE 2

30 MINUTES – Sketch ideas for a logo to go with the above name(s).

And/or rough out designs for posters to advertise specific events.

You will be surprised as to how many good ideas will come to the fore, if the atmosphere encourages creative thinking.

EXERCISE 3

30 MINUTES – Use *Prayer Pacesetting* by John Earwicker as a basis for half an hour of intercessory prayer for your planned activities. Agree together a strategy for prayer both before, during and after your outreach.

INTER-CHURCH EVANGELISM

ADVANTAGES

1. One of the biggest criticisms of the church by onlookers is that it is so divided. A united act of mission is a powerful witness. It shows that Christians can work together. It works towards Jesus' desire that 'all of them may be one'. It shows that God's love is more powerful than differences between people.

2. Two churches working together can have more effect than one on its own. More churches can have an even greater effect. There will be more resources available in terms of people, equipment and premises. There will also be more natural contacts both of the churches and of individual members.

PROBLEMS

Despite the tremendous advantages of working with other churches, we need to go into such a venture with our eyes open to the potential problems.

1. Theology. There will inevitably be different outlooks on doctrine and beliefs between various churches. Sometimes the differences will be minor, but from time to time there will be major differences. I recall one town where the desire for outreach was thwarted year after year by the failure of the Council of Churches to agree on the meaning of 'mission'!

A church's theology will affect its attitude towards evangelism and the methods it is willing to use. Some churches, mainly hard-line evangelical, will not work with others who use music or drama to present the gospel. The title of a mission can also create tensions: theological objections can result in compromise, producing almost meaingless names which fail to communicate anything about the aims of the project.

2. Follow-up. Unfortunately, successful outreach can create problems. I have been in situations where churches were so concerned about where new Christians should grow in their faith that they refused to take part in an evangelistic venture. This is a ludicrous situation: surely we should be more concerned about bringing people into God's family than about which church they attend.

3. Manpower. Although there is potentially more manpower available when more than one church is involved, inter-church evangelism can have the opposite effect. People may be less likely to involve themselves when the evangelism appears to be one stage further removed than if it were organized within their own church.

SOLUTIONS

These problem areas can be tackled by applying principles detailed in the main text of this book.

1. Theology. Obviously it is pointless to work with churches whose understanding of the gospel is diametrically opposed to our own. However, it may be profitable to encourage those churches to have a nominal involvement once the main details and arrangements have been made. People connected with such churches may even hear the gospel for the first time.

Generally, it is a good idea to work with a small group of churches who have a strong concensus of opinion about the basics of mission. This group may be the total number of churches involved or it may act as a core for a district-wide project which would enable believers from other fellowships to participate.

One option is to test the waters by organizing a single event which would act as a pilot scheme. This will give an indication of how well-disposed people are to working together. It will also give an opportunity to evaluate communication and co-operation.

2. Follow-up. Church politics should never interfere in the spiritual growth of a new Christian. There must be an overall co-ordinator of follow-up who has strong links with the follow-up co-ordinators of individual churches. The over-riding concern must always be the well-being of the new believer and enquirer, even if decisions are made which upset the hierarchy of a church.

Which churches should look after enquirers and converts? The following guidelines may be helpful. Does the person concerned have a natural contact with a particular fellowship through friend or family? Which churches are committed to discipling through tailor-made groups or one-to-one systems? Does he or she have any strong preferences?

3. Manpower. The co-ordinating body must try to use every available means to ensure that:

☐ all members own the aims and objectives for themselves,

☐ all members are fully aware of developments and arrangements,

☐ all members are encouraged to pray individually and in groups for the mission activities.

It is essential that the people who

make up the co-ordinating body are, or have close contact with, key people in each congregation who can motivate and mobilize as many other members as possible.

There are many organizations which can be used for inter-church evangelistic ventures. Apart from those based around the ministry of one particular evangelist, those that stand out are: British Youth For Christ, Saltmine and Scripture Union (see Appendix 4 for addresses). They can provide advice, resources, and personnel to work with local Christians in district-wide evangelism.

| APPENDIX 2 |

WEENIES: BIBLE STUDY WITH A DIFFERENCE

The following are extracts from *Weenies*, a series of Bible Studies for new and non-Christians, designed by Fran Morrison and not, at the time of writing, published. I include the extracts, with permission, in order to stimulate individuals to take the concepts and develop them in their own situation.
   From the Introduction:
   'Weenies is not a set of Bible Studies as such, but an approach – a way of doing things that allows the Bible to do its work with unchurched people, introducing them to truth about God in the same way that Jesus did – through storytelling, imagination and discovery.'
   The venue should be very informal to reflect the style of the sessions. Group leaders will need to prepare themselves by doing a bit of homework although sessions should be presented with a strong sense that we are all learning, including the leader. Sessions last as long as they take – that could be ten minutes or if things really get going two hours, but make sure there is no preaching. Use *only* one Bible passage per session, no cross-references or verses not set in their context.
   From Weenies 1: GOD
   'Why start with the theology of salvation when many people don't even know who God is? What does he look like? What colour is he? For a non-Christian this is a pretty good

place to start.

'Ask them to think for a moment about these questions, and then for each one in turn to say one thing about what they think God is/is like (or write them on large sheet of paper, eg reverse side of wallpaper). Make no comment other than encouraging ones, even if what they say is wrong – you have asked for their opinion, not a theological truth.'

Having explained what you are doing first, pray a very simple, brief prayer. Thank God for this opportunity to learn about him, and ask his help to do so.

'Give everybody a Bible (modern version) but ask them not to open it yet. Rather, they should imagine that they are watching the scene that you are about to describe. This scene is a passage from the Bible, an event that really happened to someone a long time before Jesus came, and they should picture it as you read it, almost as though they were watching it on a giant screen.

'Read, slowly, Isaiah 6:1–4.

'Now tell people the page number so they can look this up. Ask for a couple of impressions – strange, weird, powerful are some that may

arise. Explain that there are lots of clues in this story about what God is like, so you're now, as a group, going to look at some of them. Do this by question and answer, as follows. Encourage all answers and don't respond negatively – I've suggested some but this doesn't mean all other answers are wrong. You want people to join in and have a go even if they feel they have little to offer. . . . Listen attentively to all answers.'

Q. Why do you think it matters that it was the year King Uzziah died? (. . . ties this with real history . . . a real happening, not a made up story.)

Q. Why a throne? (shows kingship)

Q. Why high and exalted? (they raised up important people . . . eg Pope or Queen so that everyone can see – or like we do with football heroes.)

Q. What about His train filling the temple? What does it show? ((like royal wedding gown train) . . . the more glorious the clothes . . . the more important was the person wearing them. . . .)

Q. What about seraphs – what are they? (. . . explain . . .

heavenly creatures, a bit like angels.)

Q. Why did they cover their faces? (Because God is just too great to look at. . . .)

Q. Why did they cover their feet? (. . . people took their shoes off if they were on holy ground. . . .)

Q. What does 'holy' mean? Let them have a good try at this one – there'll be lots of guesses. (A good way to demonstrate the meaning of holy is to get two volunteers to hold each end of a piece of string or tape, and say 'I'm now going to make this holy'. While they wait with bated breath, you take a pair of scissors and cut it neatly in two. The root meaning of the word 'holy' is 'to cut or separate'. What it really means is that God is so different from us that he is completely separate – for example, he is completely good. Let them ponder the implications of this in their own time.)

Q. What about the temple shaking? What does it suggest to you? (Great power.)

Q. What about smoke? (. . . a screen, which stops you seeing things clearly. . . .)

Let them talk about anything else that comes out of the passage, then suggest that they close their books and read the passage to them again in the same way that you did before. Ask them, each in turn, to say one word which they feel describes God as the Bible shows him here. Don't attempt to correct anyone – they are giving their impressions, which are valuable in showing you what they think and how this passage has affected them.'

Pray something along the lines of 'Thank you God for showing us through the Bible that you are so amazing. Help us find out more'.

Make coffee, and chat some more in order to get to know each other.

Further sessions:
- ☐ Man as God made him (Genesis 1)
- ☐ What went wrong? (Genesis 3)
- ☐ Jesus – who was/is he? (Mark 6:45–51)
- ☐ Jesus – who was/is he? (Luke 4:1–13)
- ☐ Jesus – what did he do? (Isaiah 52:13 – 53:12)
- ☐ Death to life (Ephesians 2:1–10)

The key is to get into the stories (or passages using a story-telling approach) and let them speak for themselves – definitely no preaching. You can never run out of topics, in fact group members might like to suggest subjects.

| APPENDIX 3 |

RESOURCES LIST

DIRECTORIES (for speakers, artistes, and organizations)
The Masterlist (published annually), Masterplan Publishing
UK Christian Handbook (published bi-annually), MARC Europe/ Evangelical Alliance/Bible Society

TRAINING IN EVANGELISM
Evangelism: A Way of Life, Rebecca Manley Pippert/Ruth Siemens (Scripture Union, 1986) Bible study
Person to Person (Bible Society/ Scripture Union/Campus Crusade for Christ, 1987) Video-based course
Care to Say Something? (Scripture Union, 1983)
Operation Breakthrough, Jim Smith (Church Pastoral Aid Society) Youth evangelism
What I've Always Wanted to Say (Church Pastoral Aid Society)
Come Back Evangelism (Church Pastoral Aid Society)
Good News Down The Street Course (Church Pastoral Aid Society) – includes Good News Down the Street, Michael Wooderson (Grove Books)

A Man's Life (Church Pastoral Aid Society) Video-based course
Evangelism Kit (Baptist Publications)
Small Group Evangelism, Dick Peace (Scripture Union, 1987)

EVANGELISTIC MATERIAL
Knowing God Personally (Scripture Press, 1985)
Journey Into Life, Norman Warren (Falcon, 1964)
Start a New Life, David Watson (Falcon, 1979)
Road Clear, Norman Warren (Falcon, 1972)
What if I do? What if I don't?, Jim Smith (CYFA, 1982)

FOLLOW-UP MATERIAL
Adult
LIFE: New Life with Jesus Christ (Christian Publicity Organization)
GROWTH: Growing in Knowing Jesus (Christian Publicity Organization)
Considering Christ Series (Navpress, 1984)

Think It Through, George Howard (Navpress, 1984)
The Way Ahead, Norman Warren (Falcon, 1966)
Caring for New Christians (Scripture Union/Bible Society)
49 Steps, Roy Crowne (British Youth For Christ)
Now You Are A Christian, Selwyn Hughes (Marshall Pickering, 1983)

Youth
The Transformation Pack, Discovery (Campus Crusade for Christ, 1984)
Growing More Like Jesus (Church Pastoral Aid Society)
More Like Jesus (Church Pastoral Aid Society, 1981)
Go For It! (Crusaders)
Just Looking, John Allan (Bible Society/BYFC, 1987)

| APPENDIX 4 |

USEFUL ADDRESSES

ADMINISTRY
69 Sandridge Road, ST ALBANS, Herts. AL1 4AG
Materials and advice for organization and administration.

BAGSTER & TRINITY VIDEO
Westbrooke House, 76 High Street, ALTON, Hants. GU34 1EN
Sale and hire of videos.

BIBLE SOCIETY
Stonehill Green, Westlea, SWINDON, Wilts. SN5 7DG
Literature, resources and training for evangelism.

BREAK-THRU MANAGEMENT CO.
Kerygma House, Canal Road, LEEDS, W Yorks. LS12 2PL
Agency for musicians and evangelistic concerts

BRITISH CHURCH GROWTH ASSOCIATION
St Mark's Chambers, Kennington Park Road, LONDON SE11 4PW
Training and resources for understanding church growth.

BRITISH YOUTH FOR CHRIST
Cleobury Place, CLEOBURY MORTIMER, nr Kidderminster, Worcs. DY14 8JG
Personnel and resources for missions (small and large scale) and schools work.

CAMPUS CRUSADE FOR CHRIST
131 Lewes Road, BRIGHTON, W Sussex BN2 3LG
Literature and resources for evangelism.

CCA MISSION FOR HOME EVANGELISM

3 Grange Road, EGHAM, Surrey
TW20 9QW
Training and resources for door-to-door evangelism.

CHILDREN WORLDWIDE

The Wite House, High Street,
ANGMERING, Littlehampton,
W Sussex BN16 4AH
Training and resources for child evangelism.

CHRISTIAN BROADCAST TRAINING LTD

PO Box 38, NEWMARKET, Suffolk
CB8 7EG
Training in radio broadcasting.

CHRISTIAN PUBLICITY ORGANIZATION

Garcia Estate, Canterbury Road,
WORTHING, W Sussex BN13 1BW
Large range of evangelistic literature
and posters/handbills, etc for
overprinting with local details.

CHRISTIANS IN EDUCATION

16 Maids' Causeway, CAMBRIDGE
CB5 8DA
Advice on involvement in schools.

CHRISTIAN VIEWPOINT

40 Brooke Street, STOURBRIDGE, W
Midlands DY8 3XF
Resources and training for
evangelism of friends and
neighbours.

CHRISTIAN WORLD AUDIO VISUAL SERVICES

PO Box 30, 123 Deansgate,
MANCHESTER M60 3BX
Film and video library.

CHURCHES PURCHASING SCHEME (CPS RESOURCES)

Herald House, 96 Dominion Road,
WORTHING, W Sussex BN14 8JP
Resources, equipment, stationery
supplies, etc.

CHURCH PASTORAL AID SOCIETY

Falcon Court, 32 Fleet Street,
LONDON EC4Y 1DB
Resources and training materials for
evangelism.

CLEOBURY PLACE

CLEOBURY MORTIMER, nr
Kidderminster, Worcs. DY14 8HL
Residential centre for evangelism
and discipleship. Includes 'Fort
Rocky', residential theme centre.

CREATIVE PUBLISHING

Downwood, Claverton Down Road,
Claverton Down, BATH, Avon BA2
6DT
Evangelistic literature and Gospels
that can be customized for your
locality.

CRUSADE FOR WORLD REVIVAL (CWR)

Box 11, WALTON-ON-THAMES,
Surrey
Resources for evangelism and
discipling.

CTVC

Beeson's Yard, Bury Lane,
RICKMANSWORTH, Herts. WD3
1DS

Film and video library. Training in radio and TV production.

DAVID STILLMAN EVANGELISTIC ASSOCIATION
PO Box 102, READING, Berks. RG3 3NP
Personnel for evangelism in prisons.

EVANGELICAL ALLIANCE
Whitefield House, 186 Kennington Park Road, LONDON SE11 4BT
Useful for access to evangelistic organizations, resources and research.

EVANGELISM EXPLOSION
228 Shirley Road, SOUTHAMPTON, Hants. SO1 3HR
Training courses and materials for evangelism, especially door-to-door.

FULL GOSPEL BUSINESSMEN'S FELLOWSHIP INTERNATIONAL
PO Box 11, KNUTSFORD, Cheshire WA16 6QP
Resource for evangelism amongst businessmen.

INTERNATIONAL FILMS
235 Shaftesbury Avenue, LONDON WC2H 8EL
Film and video library

MARC EUROPE
Cosmos House, 6 Homesdale Road, BROMLEY, Kent BR2 9EX
Research and church management consultancy.

MISSION FOR CHRIST (RURAL EVANGELISM)
9 White Rock Road, HASTINGS, E Sussex TN34 1LE
Pesonnel and resources for evangelism in rural areas.

NAVPRESS
Tregaron House, 27 High Street, NEW MALDEN, Surrey KT3 4BY
Literature and resources for evangelism and follow-up.

OPEN AIR CAMPAIGNERS
18 Rosemary Drive, SHOREHAM-BY-SEA, W Sussex BN4 6HT
Resources for street evangelism.

PERFORMING RIGHTS SOCIETY
29/33 Berriers St, LONDON WIP 4AA
Licences for public performance of live and recorded music.

PRISON FELLOWSHIP
ENGLAND AND WALES
PO Box 263, LONDON SW1E 6HP
SCOTLAND
PO Box 366, Bishopbriggs, GLASGOW, Strathclyde G64 2RF
Evangelism to prisoners and ex-prisoners.

SALTMINE TRUST
PO Box 15, DUDLEY, W Midlands DY3 2AN
Evangelistic teams for large missions.

SCRIPTURE UNION
130 City Road, LONDON EC1V 2NJ
Personnel and resources for missions.

SCRIPTURE UNION IN SCHOOLS
130 City Road, LONDON EC1V 2NJ

Personnel and resources for schools work.

SCRIPTURE UNION TRAINING UNIT
26–30 Heathcote Street,
NOTTINGHAM NG1 3AA
Training in all aspects of missions and outreach.

SWINDON OPEN AIR PROJECT
37 Beckhampton Street, SWINDON, Wilts. SN1 2JY
Street evangelism.

THEATREWORKS
PO Box 110, MAIDSTONE, Kent ME14 4HP

Has contact with many Christian theatre companies and mime artistes

UCCF
38 De Montfort Street, LEICESTER LE1 7GP
Advice and resources for evangelism in universities and colleges.

YOUTH WITH A MISSION
13 Highfield Oval, Ambrose Lane, HARPENDEN, Herts. AL5 4BX
Personnel and training for evangelism

| APPENDIX 5 |

FURTHER READING

GENERAL
I Believe in Evangelism, David Watson (Hodder and Stoughton, 1979)
Evangelism – Now and Then, Michael Green (IVP, 1979)
Power Evangelism, John Wimber (Hodder and Stoughton, 1985)
Mission and Omission, Jim Hart (Third Way vol 10 no 7)

CHAPTER 1
PRAYER AND MOTIVATION
Prayer: Key to Revival, Paul Y Cho, Word, 1985

Prayer Pacesetting, John Earwicker (Scripture Union, 1987)
Dirty Hands, David Hall (STL/Kingsway, 1986)
Sold Out, Clive Calver (Lakeland, 1980)
Three Times Three Equals Twelve, Brian Mills (Kingsway, 1986)

CHAPTER 2
PERSONAL WITNESS
Out of the Saltshaker, Rebecca Manley Pippert (IVP, 1979)
Evangelism as a Lifestyle, Jim Petersen (Navpress, 1985)

Evangelism for Our Generation, Jim Petersen (Navpress, 1985)
Time to Share, Jim Smith (Kingsway, 1983)
How to Give Away Your Faith, Paul E Little (IVP, 1966)
The Natural Touch, Kim Swithinbank (Marshall Pickering, 1988)

Explaining Christianity

Explaining Your Faith, Alister McGrath (IVP/STL, 1988)
It Makes Sense, Stephen Gaukroger (Scripture Union, 1987)
Express Checkout, John Allan/Gus Eyre (Paternoster, 1986)

CHAPTER 3
METHODS OF EVANGELISM
A Guide to Evangelism, ed Copley, Moffat, Smith, Calver (Marshalls, 1984)
Small Group Evangelism, Richard Peace (Scripture Union, 1987)
To Reach a Nation, Gavin Reid (Hodder and Stoughton, 1987)
Know How to Run a Holiday Club, David Savage (Scripture Union, 1986)
Know How to Use your Home for Evangelism, Derek Cleave (Scripture Union, 1986)
Love Won Another, Lewis and Molly Misselbrook (Marshall Pickering, 1987)

CHAPTER 4
REACHING THE PEOPLE
Beyond the Churches, Ed Peter Brierley (EA/MARC Europe, 1984)
Urban Harvest, Roy Joslin (Evangelical Press, 1982)
A World Without Windows, Derek Tidball (Scripture Union, 1987)

CHAPTER 5
MOBILIZING THE CHURCH
Administry publish several papers relating to communication.

CHAPTER 6
PLANNING
Crowdbreakers, Bob Moffett, pp15–20 (Pickering, 1983)
Strategy for Living, Dayton & Engstrom (Regal Books)
Planning a Campaign, David Guy (Salvation Army, 1987)

CHAPTER 7
FOLLOW-UP
Disciples are Made – Not Born, Walter A Henrichsen (Victor – a division of Scripture Press, 1974)
Go and Make Apprentices, Philip Vogel (Kingsway, 1986)
The ABC of Follow-Up, Ron Smith (STL, 1974)

CHAPTER 8
ORGANIZING ACTIVITIES
The Complete Youth Manual Vol 1, Steve Chalke (Kingsway, 1987)